Our Escape from Nazi-Occupied Norway:

Norwegian Resistance to Nazism

By Leif Terdal

Trafford
PUBLISHING™

Edited by Marge Terdal, PhD
Cover Design/Artwork by Thad Hendrickson

Note for Librarians: A cataloguing record for this book is available from Library
and Archives Canada at www.collectionscanada.ca/amicus/index-e.html

Printed in Victoria, BC, Canada.

ISBN: 978-1-4251-7727-0

*We at Trafford believe that it is the responsibility of us all, as both individuals
and corporations, to make choices that are environmentally and socially sound.
You, in turn, are supporting this responsible conduct each time you purchase a
Trafford book, or make use of our publishing services. To find out how you are
helping, please visit www.trafford.com/responsiblepublishing.html*

*Our mission is to efficiently provide the world's finest, most comprehensive
book publishing service, enabling every author to experience success.
To find out how to publish your book, your way, and have it available
worldwide, visit us online at www.trafford.com/10510*

www.trafford.com

North America & international
toll-free: 1 888 232 4444 (USA & Canada)
phone: 250 383 6864 ♦ fax: 250 383 6804
email: info@trafford.com

The United Kingdom & Europe
phone: +44 (0)1865 487 395   local rate: 0845 230 9601
facsimile: +44 (0)1865 481 507   mail: info.uk@trafford.com

10 9 8 7 6 5 4 3 2

Dedication

To Marge, Paul, and Erik

To Harriet Hansen Terdal, and the four men of the Norwegian resistance who helped us to escape:

Dr. Sigurd Hus

Ola Olsen

Nils Nessa, crew of the *Siglaos*

Captain Brevik of the ss *Brant County*

Leif Terdal was our Classmate & Colleague at Taylor Univ. Class of

CONTENTS

PREFACE

Was there a clue, a warning of any kind, that Norway would bear the second brunt (after Poland) of Nazi Germany's horrific blitzkrieg of their offensive in WW II? That question has troubled me since childhood. Should my parents have known of the impending disaster and prepared for it? Did the Norwegian government have reason to believe that their country would face a massive attack and then be occupied by a Nazi military that utterly stifled basic human rights? The British and French governments were quick to send troops to Norway to fight the Germans, but did they anticipate the German attack? Had they anticipated the attack, could they have been able to prevent or thwart the invasion? Did the American government have a clue?

Furthermore, WHY? Why did the Germans attack a small neutral country of three million people, and then occupy the country with 350,000 troops? One German soldier for every nine Norwegians! Why did Germany maintain a military force of that magnitude even after they invaded Russia in June 1941, and even after Germany was short of troops after the D-Day invasion in June 1944? How did the Norwegians resist, and at what cost?

My parents were Norwegians who emigrated to the U.S. in the early 1920's. My father, Alf Terdal, came from a small industrial town of Rubbestadneset on the island of Bomlo on the west coast of Norway about 60 miles south of Bergen. My father was a diesel engineer and had the papers to qualify him to be a chief engineer on ships. All it took for him to enter the United States in the 1920's was to arrive aboard any foreign ship, then walk away from the ship and apply for a job as a seaman aboard a U.S. vessel. At the turn of the century there was such a shortage of qualified seamen to man U.S. ships that Congress passed a law to that effect. The foreign ship owner was prohibited by U.S. law to compel a seaman to return to the ship where he had been employed. It was to the advantage of a foreign seaman, now in the United States, to become a U.S. citizen. He could then more easily move up in rank and earn the level of employment that met his qualifications. So my father went through the process of becoming a U.S. citizen.

My mother, whose maiden name was Harriet Hansen, was born and raised in the southern city of Arendal. She also came to New York in the early 1920's along with her two sisters. Each in turn married a Norwegian immigrant all connected with seamanship and shipping. All three families had social and religious activities connected with the Norwegian Bethelship Methodist church in Brooklyn, New York. My mother did not have the economic incentive, as did my father, so she did not apply for U.S. citizenship during her initial stay in the U.S.

My parents were married in 1932 and their first child, a son named Roy, was born in September 1933. I was born the day after Christmas in 1937. My parents had already decided to return to Norway because my father believed that he would have better income potential in Norway than in the throes of the depression in the U.S. They waited to leave for Norway by ship until June 1938, when I was six months old. We were to return by sea nearly four years later to escape Nazi-occupied Norway.

In some ways a war experience is similar to a stone thrown with great force onto a body of water. When the stone hits it skips, and skips again and again, sending ripples of small waves across the water. As a child I enjoyed throwing rocks on water to make them skip. My record was a stone I threw that skipped 27 distinct times before it quietly sank. The time frame of the stone throw may have lasted 15 to 20 seconds. In contrast the ripple effects of the German invasion of Norway on April 9th, 1940 are still in motion. The Third Reich did not last 1000 years. It ended in May 1945. However, the stone that hit the water in 1940 will still have its impact for more than 1000 years. This book is about how the impact of the April 9th invasion of Norway affected one family.

Part I

**THE MILITARY DEFEAT
OF NORWAY:**

**TERMS OF THE
OCCUPATION**

Chapter 1

RETURNING "HOME" TO NORWAY, EXPECTING PEACE NOT WAR

My parents returned to Norway from the United States in June 1938. They had emigrated from Norway to the U.S. in the 1920's and met through the Bethelship Norwegian Methodist Church in Brooklyn, N.Y. After they married, my father, Alf, worked as a chief engineer on ships and my mother, Harriet, was a homemaker. My father took out U.S. citizenship because it enabled him to get better positions within the shipping industry.

The United States was so short of experienced seamen in the early part of the Twentieth Century, that any foreign seaman could walk off his ship and be protected by US authorities from being forced to return to the ship of his employment bearing a foreign flag. By an Act of Congress, known as the La Follette-Furuseth Law of March 1915, the United States was able to hire enough capable seamen from Europe to man US merchant ships. 1

My mother seeing no reason to do so, did not take out US citizenship. My parents both thought they would return to Norway. My older brother, Roy, was born in 1933 and I was born the day after Christmas in 1937. Since my father was a seaman he was not home during the late stage of his wife's pregnancy. When my mother felt the baby was due, she took a cab to the hospital where I was born.

In June 1938 our family moved back to Norway and settled in the town of Rubbestadneset on the Island of Bomlo, where my father had been raised. Rubbestaddneset is on the west coast of Norway about sixty miles south of Bergen. Although on the southwest coast of Norway, Bomlo is at latitude 60, a bit further north than Glacier Bay, Alaska.

My parents were informed and well-read but had no idea that Norway would be attacked by Germany. They were concerned about the horrific German invasion of Poland in September 1939. The German blitzkrieg attack rendered Poland helpless in sixteen days. During the mopping up of local resistance, eastern Poland was invaded and occupied by Russia.

Prior to the German invasion of Poland, my parents like other citizens in Norway were deeply troubled by *Kristallnacht (November 9-10, 1938)*. This was the horrific assault on Jewish communities in Germany. During the deadly and destructive attack more than one thousand synagogues and many thousands of Jewish places of business were destroyed and 35,000 Jews were arrested. Many other Jews were physically assaulted, causing death and injuries. Police, fire department and ambulances did not respond.[2] Furthermore the Christian churches in Germany remained silent and failed to voice opposition to the assault on the Jewish community. Clergy and church leaders who might have protested and offered help to the Jewish community had previously been arrested and imprisoned by the thousands (both Protestant and Catholic) for not supporting Adolf Hitler and his policies.

My parents were well aware that both England and France declared war against Germany after the German attack and before the swift military defeat of Poland. But no direct fighting had yet occurred following the declaration of war. Both my parents listened daily to Norwegian and British news accounts of what might occur next, but they did not expect Norway to be attacked.

Russia attacked Finland on November 30, 1939, and after suffering huge losses the Russians overcame the comparatively small but effective Finnish army. Finland bordered Norway in the north and the Russian invasion was very disturbing to Norwegians and to my parents. Some wondered if Russia had eyes on invading Norway.

There were, in fact, three important events that led up to the timing of the German invasion of Norway. They are the *Altmark* incident, the April 5th "Peace Dinner," and the three men who had an inside track to Adolf Hitler and who urged him to invade and occupy Norway.

The Altmark *Incident*

The *Altmark*, a German auxiliary of the *Graf Spee*, was a floating prison ship and had on board 299 British merchant seamen from British ships sunk in the South Atlantic. The *Graf Spee* was one of three modern and heavily armed pocket battle ships built by the German navy for the explicit purpose of destroying British merchant ships in the Atlantic. The other two such major warships were the *Deutchland* (renamed *Lutzow in 1940)*, and *Scheer.* In a period of about two months the *Graf Spee* sank the following nine merchant ships: *Clement, Newton Beach, Ashlea, Huntsman, Trevanion, Africa Shell, Doric Star, Tairoa and the Streonshalh.* Recognizing the severe threat to essential British shipping, the Admiralty in conjunction with the French Navy sent eight naval groups to hunt down and destroy the threat. Commander Henry Harwood RN had command of three light cruisers, HMS *Ajax,* HMS *Achilles* and HMNZS *Exeter.* In an ensuing battle the *Exeter* suffered severe damage. The *Graf Spee* suffered moderate damage and the death of about forty of her crew. Commander Hans Langsdorff, decided to withdraw to the harbor on the River Platt in Montevideo in Uruguayan waters. The British sent "secret" messages that powerful British naval reinforcements were about to arrive at the River Platt. The British sent the messages in such a way as to make sure that the Germans intercepted them. The messages were intercepted by Commander Hans Langsdorff who proceeded to send his new warship, now damaged, just beyond the harbor and had it scuttled on December 17, 1939. He committed suicide two days later, after learning that he had scuttled his ship based on faulty intelligence. The British reinforcements were days away, and Langsdorff could likely have run *Graf Spee,* though damaged, back north all the way to Germany for repairs.

The *Altmark* had been a supply ship for the *Graf Spee* and also had picked up about 300 survivors of the nine merchant ships that had been sunk. After hiding for two months off South America, the captain made an attempt to return to Germany. The British intelligence tracked the vessel and located it in February 1940. The *Altmark* had taken refuge in a fjord near Stavanger, Norway. When Winston Churchill received the information, he ordered the *Altmark* to be boarded by British navy ships and the prisoners rescued. The British naval ship *Cossack* entered the Fjord and was at first approached by the Norwegian gunboat *Kjell*. The Norwegian captain told the captain of the *Cossack* that he had boarded the *Altmark* twice and that it was unarmed and carried no weapons. Captain Phillip Viann of the *Cossack* replied that he was going to board the *Altmark* and proceeded to approach the vessel. The *Altmark* ran aground and was boarded by crew from the British vessel. A fierce fight followed which left four Germans dead and five wounded. The British discovered weapons on board and the 299 British prisoners. The prisoners had been hidden, including some in an empty oil tank. The British viewed the rescue as a major victory and it was broadcast as such by British radio. 3

Even without hearing of the attack and rescue on BBC or Norwegian radio, my father would have heard of it from his contacts with maritime crew on fishing boats or docks from the area. Stavanger is not far from Rubbestadneset.

The loss was more than Adolf Hitler could tolerate, and he erupted into a violent rage. First he lost the *Graf Spee* which he had expected to devastate British shipping in the South Atlantic, and now the prisoners carried on the *Altmark* were snatched away. 4 Only one person in Norway knew that Adolf Hitler would set an exact date for the German invasion of Norway, after learning that Norway stood by passively as the British attacked and boarded the *Altmark*. That man was Vidkun Quisling.

The April Fifth "Peace Dinner"

In her memoirs of her service as U.S. Ambassador to Norway, Florence Harriman wrote of an invitation she received along with other officials of the Norwegian Foreign Office. Each received on a formal engraved card, from the German Minister, an invitation to view a "peace film." The dinner and film would take place that evening, "full dress and orders to be worn." The film they saw was a terrifying documentary of the bombing and utter destruction of the city of Warsaw, Poland, filmed during the September 1939 German blitzkrieg. There was no discussion for the stunned guests, and no question and answer period followed the program. The German official quietly explained that the "peace film" showed what would happen to any country that resisted Nazi attempts to defend it from England. The shocked audience of Norwegian and foreign diplomats wondered why the film had been shown to *them.* 5 In four days (April 9, 1940) they would know.

Men Who Urged Hitler to Invade and Occupy Norway

Three men were instrumental in convincing Hitler that Germany must invade and occupy Norway. 6

Admiral Raeder, Chief of the Naval Staff, submitted a series of papers to Adolf Hitler on October 10, 1939, under a heading "Gaining of Bases in Norway." He stressed the disadvantage of the British occupying Norway where they could block German approaches to the Baltic. Since the German industry was almost 100 percent dependent on the import of Swedish steel, the Norwegian port of Narvik had to be in German control. He also stressed the importance of access to Norwegian territory, including the fjords for the planned attack on Britain.

Admiral Rosenberg, the foreign affairs expert of the Nazi Party, visualized Scandinavia as a Nordic community that embraced the pure race ideals of the Nazi party. Rosenberg knew of Vidkun Quisling, a former secretary of war in Norway, and a pro-Nazi. He invited Quisling to meet Hitler.

Quisling met Hitler on December 14, 1939, and discussed a

possible German invasion and occupation of Norway. He told Hitler that he was head of a pro-nazi party in Norway (Nasjonal Samling) and of his concern that England would attack Norway. He also expressed his personal hatred for Stalin and the Russians. Although he gave no assurances to Quisling of any military plans by Germany, after the meeting Hitler ordered plans to be developed (code name Weserubung) for an attack and occupation of Norway.

Level of Norwegian Military Preparedness Prior to the Attack on Norway

The peace time Norwegian Military (prior to April 9, 1940) consisted of 7,000 men. The army, however, had not conducted field training, and most recruits had not even met their commanders. As for equipment, the military had vintage cannons and obsolete 6.5 Krag-Jurgenson rifles. The Norwegian army had no sub-machine guns, no grenades and no anti-aircraft guns. They had one army tank and a few airplanes.

The Royal Norwegian Navy had a small number of vessels. The two largest ones *Norge* and *Eidsvold*, were the oldest naval worships in Europe. The Norwegian navy had not left port on training missions since 1918. 7 Norway was not a poor country; Norwegians had a large and modern merchant fleet and a large commercial fishing fleet. Norway was simply not prepared for war.

Oslo, the capital of Norway, was protected by the Fortress of Oscarsborg which overlooked Oslo Fjord. The fortress then and now is an outstanding tourist site. At the time of the outbreak of new and widespread military aggression, the fortress of Oscarsborg was equipped with ancient nineteenth century Krupp cannons.

Government of Norway Prior to the Attack of April 9, 1940

Norwegians in 1935 elected a government that promised economic and social reforms and was committed to neutrality regarding international affairs. They assumed that their declaration of neutrality and their membership in the League of Nations would keep them out of war. 8 Citizens throughout Europe remembered the horrific losses sustained in World War I. Many countries lost an entire generation of men, and caused many people to believe that war should be avoided at all cost. At the time Norway was attacked the leaders of the Norwegian government were the following: 9

Johan Nygaardsvold was the prime minister. He supported social policies including education, health and economic security for Norwegian citizens. He was not interested in military or defense matters.

Halvadon Koht was the foreign minister. An eminent historian, he was confident that international law and the League of Nations would protect Norway's explicit statement of neutrality.

Trygve Lie, the Minister of Justice, was an effective statesman. He later became the first Secretary-General of the United Nations.

Carl Fredric Monsen, a pacifist and conscientious objector, was the Defense Minister.

One may wonder why a nation would appoint a pacifist as Secretary of Defense. Remember, the U.S. appointed James Watt to the position of Secretary of the Interior where he could be as lax as he and the President wanted in "protecting" the environment of our forests, National Parks, and other natural resources. James Watt, as Secretary of the Interior, protected industry from what he viewed as excessive restrictions brought on by environmentalists. The rationale in Norway was the same, but with the opposite twist. As the Secretary of Defense, Carl Monsen restricted the allocation of valuable national resources for the military, which permitted the resources to be used for the health and education for the citizens of Norway.

Prince Charles of Denmark, son-in-law of King Edward VII of England, was elected King of Norway in 1905 when Norway became independent of Swedish control. Prince Charles took the name King Haakon VII. The choice of title was appropriate.

The last king of independent Norway was King Haakon VI (1355-1380). After his death and a horrific national tragedy of the Black Death, Norway entered into a union with Denmark. The Black Death, which hit Norway in the mid 1300's killed up to 80 percent of the population. Because the death toll was so extensive and had occurred in a period of just a few years, Norwegians were left without the resources for self government. Some communities were totally wiped out, and remained uninhabited for as long as 200 years. Denmark, aware of the catastrophic disaster, agreed to govern Norway and that arrangement lasted about four hundred years.10

The arrangement with Denmark ended by order of the British in 1814, after the British victory over France in the Napoleonic war. (Denmark had sided with France, and for that Denmark was to be punished). By the Peace of Kiel in January 1814, the Danish King ceded Norway to the King of Sweden.11 Sweden yielded to a strong nationalistic movement in Norway, thus permitting Norway to become an independent nation in 1905.

King Haakon VII had been a Naval Admiral and he was very tuned into foreign and military affairs. He had made a comment to Winston Churchill in 1932, that if Adolf Hitler achieved and retained power, he would start a war engulfing Europe. King Haakon VII, however, could not veto the decisions of the Prime Minister and his cabinet. Nevertheless, he was very popular and respected by the citizens of Norway and exerted tremendous influence when war came. 12

The British Micro-invasion of Norwegian Territory

Winston Churchill was appointed First Lord of the Admiralty by Neville Chamberlain shortly after Germany invaded Poland. One of his first actions was to recommend to Neville Chamberlain and British military leaders that shipments of Swedish iron be blocked and prevented from reaching Germany. He had ample reason to have recommended such a policy. The British Minister of Economic Warfare informed Churchill that a total blockage of Swedish ore to Germany would end Germany's ability to wage war after just a few months. 13

The French Premier Edouard Daladier shared the concern of German access to Swedish ore. He agreed to work with the British government to work out a military option to block Swedish ore from reaching the vast German military industrial complex.

Norway became a strategic focus for both Germany and the Allies. A vast portion of Swedish ore for export was shipped by rail from Sweden to the ice-free port of Narvik, Norway – a distance of only about thirty miles. Although Narvik is well north of the Arctic Circle, the deep harbor is ice-free all winter long.

Neville Chamberlain blocked every possible idea of a military move against Norway. He once said he would agree to a task force taking control of the Port of Narvik, if the military agreed they would not fire a shot at a Norwegian in the case of a Norwegian counter-attack.

On April 8, 1940, the British sent a few naval ships to Narvik and laid out some mines to present a hazard to German vessels approaching or leaving Narvik. 14 The war began in Norway the next day.

Chapter 2

GERMANY ATTACKS NORWAY: APRIL 9, 1940

Hitler had ordered the attack on Norway to focus on the six major ports of Norway by a coordinated effort by Navy, Airforce and Army and to begin simultaneously before dawn on April 9, 1940. Several hours before the attack, the German diplomat, Kurt Brauer, who was stationed in Oslo, was prepared to meet with the Norwegian government (on very short notice) and to demand an immediate and unconditional surrender. The actual wording of Hitler's directive is instructive:

Latest developments of the Scandinavian situation render it imperative that all preparations be made for an occupation of Denmark and Norway by units of the Wehrmacht. This will enable us to forestall British actions in Scandinavia and the Baltic, to safeguard our supplies of iron ore from Sweden, and to improve the starting positions of our naval and air forces against Great Britain. (…) It is of the utmost importance that both the Nordic countries and the Allies be caught unawares by our operation. All preparations must take this element into account. 1

Hitler added the following instruction:

In the course of Weserubung, (the code name for the attack on Norway and Denmark) *all political measures to be taken in regard to the governments of Denmark and Norway, as well as German interventions in the administration and economy of both countries, are to conform with the requirements of a peaceful occupation, having as its aim the protection of the Nordic countries' neutrality. Great pains should be taken to dissuade the Danish and Norwegian governments from offering armed resistance, and to persuade them to accept a German occupation.* 2

The six major ports along the vast Norwegian coastline targeted for the German onslaught were the following:

Group I, Narvik, consisting of 2,000 men trained to fight under mountain and snow conditions embarked in ten destroyers, escorted by the battle cruisers *Scharnhorst* and *Gneisenau.*

Group II, Trondheim, consisting of 1,700 men, embarked in four destroyers, escorted by the heavy cruiser *Admiral Hipper.* These two naval groups left German ports on April 7 and sailed at top speed for the two distant Norwegian ports. Trondheim is just below the Arctic Circle along the west coast of Norway, and Narvik is north of the Arctic Circle.

Group III, Bergen, transported 1,300 men aboard the cruisers *Koln* and *Konigsberg,* and two destroyers.

Group IV, Kristiansand, and group V, Egersund, carried troops aboard the cruiser *Karlsruhe,* the escort vessel *Tsing Tau,* three torpedo-boats and four minesweepers. These three naval groups III, IV, and V left German ports on April 8 followed later in the day by:

Group VI, Oslo, led by the heavy cruiser *Blucher,* carried a large military attachment and German government officials with the assignment of ensuring that the King of Norway and the Norwegian government either surrendered immediately or were captured. The cruiser *Blucher* was accompanied by the cruisers *Lutzow* and *Emden* and three destroyers transporting additional shock troops, Gestapo agents and high ranking government officials. 3

About 3:00 A.M., April 9, the Norwegian Prime Minister, Halv-dan Koht, was summoned for a most urgent meeting by the German diplomat Kurt Brauer, who brought with him a nineteen-page document and demanded unconditional surrender. Brauer was firm in his approach and tried to convince Koht that the German invasion, now under way, was to protect Norway from the British and the French. He stressed that resistance by Norway was futile and would be suppressed by overwhelming German military forces. Koht, however, was an expert in international affairs and aware of the Nazi capacity for deceit and terror. He asked for time to meet with the other members of the Norwegian Government to explain the German demands. A short time later, Koht returned and informed Brauer that Norway would reject the German demands. Brauer replied, "…we will be at war," to which Koht answered, "We are already at war!" 4

As they departed, the large German heavy cruiser, *Blucher*, was aflame and drifting aimlessly down the Oslo Fjord, in full view of the citizens of Oslo. Two rounds from the ancient cannons of the old fortress of Oscarsborg designed to protect Oslo had struck two fatal blows to the *Blucher*. Aircraft fuel on board the large naval vessel was ignited and the second shell struck an ammunition magazine on board causing repeated and devastating explosions. The sinking of the *Blucher* temporarily halted the attack on Oslo as the remaining German vessels and military personnel immediately began a frantic search, rescue and recovery effort. 5 The delay provided the King of Norway and the government about six hours of time to escape Oslo.

The King and members of the Parliament began a hurried escape from Oslo to Hamar, eighty miles north of Oslo. 6 In their rush to evacuate and avoid capture they failed to make a proclamation to the nation. At the railroad station a news reporter, sensing the national crisis, spoke with Koht, who explained what he knew of the scope of the German invasion. The headline news report that followed and spread throughout Norway was the only "call to arms."7 The Norwegian military mobilized immediately, without waiting for official notice from the Norwegian military command. The German invasion of Norway was followed simultaneously by news that Denmark had also been invaded. To the dismay of all patriotic Norwegians came the word that the government of Denmark had surrendered to the Germans almost immediately and essentially without firing a shot. 8

At 7:30 p.m. Vidkun Quisling entered the Norwegian government radio station in Oslo and delivered the following speech to his countrymen:

Fellow Norwegians! By laying mines in Norwegian territorial waters, England has violated the neutrality of Norway, without calling forth more than a feeble protest from the Nygaardsvold government. The German government have offered their assistance to the government of Norway, together with the solemn assurances that our national independence would be respected. ...the Nygaardsvold government have called a general mobilization and given all Norwegian military forces the senseless order to oppose German assistance by force of arms. This government then fled, after having rashly imperilled the destiny of the country and its inhabitants. Under the circumstances, the NasjonalSamling (NS) has both the right and the duty to assume the responsibility of power. .... Under present circumstances, all resistance is not only senseless, but also criminal, for it imperils the life and property of our fellow countrymen. All civil servants, all municipal employees, all land, air, naval and coastal artillery officers are duty-bound to obey the orders of the new government. Any failure to do so would ... expose the transgressor to the full rigors of justice.9

Before ending his speech Quisling announced himself as the head of government and also the Foreign Minister. In his address to the people of Norway, Quisling failed to mention that in the past December, just four months earlier, he personally visited

Adolf Hitler in Germany and urged him to invade and occupy Norway.

April 10 – 14 The potential for a stunning Allied Advance.

The day after the invasion German forces continued to arrive in Norway to further strengthen their hold on Norway. The Norwegian forces, who had not yet heard a word from General Laake, their Commander and Chief, began to assemble and position themselves.10 Across Norway, many young Norwegian men went to recruiting stations to volunteer to fight for their country. Many were turned away, some in tears, because the Norwegian Army had no uniforms or weapons to give them. Only forty thousand of all who tried to volunteer were accepted.

The naval situation was quite different. On April 10, a massive British Naval attack at Narvik by five powerful British Destroyers destroyed much of the German fleet. On the same day British dive bombers attacked and sank the German destroyer *Konigsberg* at Bergen. On April 11, a British submarine sank the cruiser *Karlsruhe* and several transports and severely damaged the pocket battleship *Lutzow*. On April 13, the British battleship *Warspite* and nine destroyers entered Ofotfjord and destroyed the remaining German destroyers at Narvik.11 The British naval victories, especially at Narvik, clearly created an opportunity for a decisive military strike at Narvik. In Narvik the Germans who survived the sinking of their ships had to be rescued and brought on land under severe weather conditions of a protracted blinding snow storm. This required a prolonged and difficult effort which made them especially vulnerable against a surprise attack.

Back in Oslo, the German diplomat Brauer, had received instruction to make one more attempt to contact the fleeing King Haakon and to have him personally reconsider "the sensible German proposal." Kurt Brauer managed to get word to the Norwegian Foreign Minister, Halvdan Koht, who had the day before announced to the German diplomat that Norway rejected the German demands. But they agreed to meet in the town of Elverum, a short distance from Nybergsund, where the Norwegian government was in hiding.

In a most improbable meeting, the German diplomat met with both King Haakon and Halvdan Koht and reiterated the point that Germany had invaded Norway to protect Norway from the British. He then stated that Germany had no confidence in the Norwegian government under Nygaardsvold. Brauer than asked if King Haakon would appoint Major Quisling as Chief of Government in Norway. His words were as follows: "The German government demanded that the King appoint Major Quisling as Chief of Government, and as ministers the men he had named in his proclamation, to whom some other personalities might be added."12 King Haakon answered that "he could not appoint a government that did not enjoy the confidence of the Norwegian people, and several elections had shown that Major Quisling did not enjoy such confidence to a sufficient degree. His government would be nothing more that a Kuusinen government."13 (Note: Otto Vilhelm Kuusinen was a Finnish communist who sided with Russia after the Russian attack on Finland. His name became a synonym for traitor). King Haakon then said he would discuss the matter with the legal Norwegian government and that Brauer would be informed by telephone that evening after he returned to his office in Oslo. What made the meeting so improbable was that Brauer, the German diplomat, was ordered to get either a statement of surrender from the King of Norway or have him arrested. Instead, he allowed him to think about it and consult with the Norwegian government.

The evening of April 10, King Haakon met with the Nygaardvold government in Nybergsund and opened the meeting with the following words:

I am profoundly moved at the idea of having to assume personal responsibility for the woes that will befall our country and our people if German demands are rejected. It is such a heavy responsibility that I shudder to bear it. The government is free to decide, but I shall make my own position clear: I cannot accept the German demands. This would conflict with everything I have considered to be my duty as a king ever since I came to Norway almost thirty-five years ago. . . . I have endeavoured to embody a constitutional monarch that was entirely loyal to the people who elected me in 1905. . . . I cannot name Quisling Prime Minister, because he has neither the confidence of the people nor that of their deputies. As a result, should the government choose to bow before the German demands, I would understand their motivations perfectly, in view of the imminent peril now threatening, and the prospect of seeing so many young Norwegians sacrifice their lives in this war; yet I would then have no other alternative than to abdicate. 14

That evening at 8 p.m. Brauer called Koht on the telephone. Koht told the German diplomat that King Haakon would not appoint a Quisling cabinet. Brauer asked if the Norwegian resistance would continue, and Koht answered, "Yes!" 15

Also on April 10, the Norwegian government removed General Laake from his post and appointed Colonel Otto Ruge to be Commander in Chief of the Norwegian military. 16

The Allied Strategy

The British naval success at Narvik, occurring within days of the German invasion, created a sense of optimism for allied forces of British, French and Polish troops who were being rushed to Norway to fight the Germans. The hastily drawn plans called for a large force of allied troops to land at Narvik and retake it from German control. However, Narvik could only be secured if allied forces also gained control of critical supply routes to Narvik. This was to be accomplished by a simultaneous massive allied attack by army and navy forces to take Trondheim away from German control. The plan to retake Trondheim consisted of British, French and Polish troops to land at Namsos and proceed to march about one hundred and thirty-five miles south to reach Trondheim.

Another large force was to land at Aandalsnes about one hundred miles south of Trondheim and proceed to march north. The two forces would form a pincer movement towards Trondheim in coordination with a massive British naval attack against German forces already positioned in Trondheim. 17

The British General Carton de Wiart was promised a substantial force to arrive at Namsos to enable him to undertake his difficult mission. The 146th Brigade was to arrive at Namsos on April 15, the 148th Brigade on the 17th, and two French Battalions on April 18. As the troops arrived in the midst of a German air raid, the small Norwegian fishing port was unable to handle the large ships, which were then unloaded at a very slow pace by small craft. The military supplies that accompanied the troops lacked skis and snow shoes, which were necessary in the winter conditions that prevailed in this part of Norway. The German air raids also damaged some of the supplies and damaged some of the naval vessels. 18

Colonel Getz, commanding officer of the Norwegian 5th Brigade, offered assistance with his detachment of Norwegian ski troops and additional ski equipment for the British. Three battalions of French troops arrived at Namsos on the night of April 19. These French soldiers were trained to fight in snow and mountain conditions, but their equipment was destroyed as was the town of Namsos by a massive German air attack on April 21. 19

The troops under the command of General Carton de Wiart (without the French) began their long advance towards Trondheim. On April 23 these forces, along with Norwegian troops led by Colonel Getz, were attacked by German mountain troops and had to withdraw back towards the bombed out town of Namsos. 20

The German attack against the forces of General de Wiart was made possible by a complete breakdown in the allied plans. On April 20 the plan for the massive naval attack on Trondheim was cancelled, and the abrupt change was made without informing General de Wiart. The reason for the change of plans was fear the British navy would be too vulnerable to German air attacks. In the complete absence of British naval forces in the vicinity of Trondheim, a German destroyer and one torpedo-boat entered safely into Trondheimfjord and landed the German troops. That completely stopped the allied forces led by General de Wiart. 21

The military situation at Aandalsnes was much worse. The Norwegian Colonel David Thue witnessed British troops in Aandalsnes who marched with four soccer balls and 50,000 cigarettes. He added this description to his government: "Very young lads who appeared to come from the slums of London. They had taken a very close interest in the women of Romsdal, and engaged in wholesale looting of stores and houses. (…) Besides, they would run like hares at the first sound of an aircraft." 22

J.M. Addis in a Foreign Office report dated 14/6/1940 wrote of the British forces at Aandalsnes: "Drunk British troops had on one occasion quarrelled and eventually fired upon some Norwegian fishermen. Again, some of the British Army officers had behaved 'with the arrogance of Prussians' and the Naval Officers were in general so cautious and suspicious that they treated every Norwegian as a Fifth Columnist and refused to believe vital information when it was given them." 23

Early on April 28, the order was given that all Allied forces in Central and Southern Norway were to evacuate. 24 Later that day German Luftwaffe bombed the cities of Aandalsnes, Molde and Kristiansund around the clock and utterly destroyed them, leaving them in smoldering ruins.

King Haakon and the members of the Norwegian government had been hiding in the small city of Molde. The British diplomat Sir Cecil Dormer received an order to evacuate the King of Norway and the Norwegian government, and to do so without telling them that the allied forces were withdrawing all forces in Central and Southern Norway. The message Dormer received:

His Majesty the King of Norway, his entourage and members of the Norwegian Government should be evacuated with last Allied troops to leave Molde area, and if necessary, this is to be done even against the King's wishes so that he may not – repeat not – fall into German hands. (…) His Majesty should not – repeat not – be informed of evacuation plan at present, and force should only be resorted to after first night of evacuation if King then refuses to leave. 25

That evening, several cars with the King, members of the Norwegian government and ministers of France, Poland and the United Kingdom who also had offices tucked in the small city of Molde escaped to the port and boarded the cruiser *Glasgow*, departed the burning city, and headed for the ultra-rural town of Tromso in the far northern reaches of Norway.

Colonel Getz and his Norwegian troops had been deployed amidst the Allied forces and were following the last orders which he received on April 26 to advance towards Steinkjer en route to the siege against Trondheim (which unbeknown to him had been cancelled). By May 2 he had no further contact with Allied forces and was surrounded by German troops. He and his troops began their retreat to Namsos. When they arrived at Namsos they found the ruins of the town and smoldering burnt out wrecks of Allied military trucks, as well as abandoned anti-aircraft guns and 300 rifles without ammunition. He found a note left by General de Wiart: "We are leaving a quantity of material here, which I hope you can come and take, and know it will be of value to you and your gallant force."26 Completely abandoned by Allied forces and without ammunition, Colonel Getz was forced to surrender his small contingent of Norwegian troops to the German forces at Namsos on May 3, 1940.

Why were Norwegian government and military officials kept in the dark about Allied war plans in Norway?

British Prime Minister Neville Chamberlain was aware of the traitorous actions of Vidkun Quisling. However, Chamberlain made the incorrect assumption that many, perhaps most, Norwegians shared the views of Quisling. In fact, Quisling never got more than 2 percent of Norwegians to side with his pro-Nazi views. In contrast, the German diplomat, Kurt Brauer, showed better judgement and recognized the outrage that most Norwegians had towards Quisling. He urged Hitler to withdraw Quisling from any prominent position in the German takeover of Norway. Quisling was removed from his self-appointed central stage position by order of Adolf Hitler, on the advice of Bauer, on April 15. 27 Chamberlain's error in judgement about the influence of Quisling was unfortunate and costly in the defense of Norway.

But the disaster of the Allied Forces in Central and Southern Norway requires more explanation. The time available for planning military action in Norway favored the Germans. The Germans began urgent strategic plans for their invasion of Norway in December 1939. That gave German military strategists four months to learn the geography of Norway and its infrastructure, including port facilities, railroad lines and roads. They learned about winter conditions and the requirements for gear and expertise with skis and snowshoes. The Germans also had time to plan for an expected Allied offensive to establish control of such critical port cities as Narvik and Trondheim. In contrast, the Allied forces began planning a counter-attack essentially the day the Germans invaded Norway.

The Allied forces were woefully unprepared for every aspect of their mission and they lacked trust in the Norwegians, who both wanted and were able to help them. The lack of planning resulted in supplies being sent in ships that could not unload at critical ports such as Namsos. British, French and Polish troops were not equipped with winter clothing or with skis and snowshoes. French commanders could not speak English, and, except for the British General de Wiart, the British did not speak French. The unfortunate collapse of discipline reported among Allied troops who were landed at Aandalsnes may well have been due to what would happen to any army of young men who are landed in foreign soil only to find that their mission had been cancelled and they received no further instruction.

Chapter 3
THE BATTLE FOR NARVIK

At this point in the war (mid-April 1940), my parents like other Norwegians had no clear, accurate information about the German invasion of Norway or what the future held. The radio and press were already controlled by the Nazis. Vidkun Quisling was not trusted by his fellow Norwegians, and his pompous address to the nation and his dismissal of King Haakon and the Norwegian government were seen, correctly, as absolute proof that Quisling was a traitor. What my mother later wrote of the military phase of the war was approximately accurate and brief. Her brevity was due to the extreme lack of reliable information about the reasons behind the German invasion and details of the fighting. Amidst the uncertainty, she wrote the following:

We were awakened in the early morning of April 9, 1940, by airplanes flying low and circling around our little community located on the island of Bomlo, off the western coast of Norway.

For several days we had heard rumors about the German fleet in the North Sea, but few believed anyone would invade the neutral, peace-loving Norway; however, the planes we saw were German. Soon we learned that the Germans had indeed invaded Norway. Although unprepared, the Norwegians fought and many died for their country. England and France sent troops who landed and fought at several parts of Norway, but soon they had to retreat. The Germans were too powerful and after a few weeks had taken over the country.
Living in an enemy-occupied country can never be fully understood if not experienced. The Nazi's initial step was to seize the newspapers and the radio stations, and from then on we were fed with their lies and distorted truths. 1

As I write this book, some 65 years after our escape, my focus remains the escape of our family from Nazi-occupied Norway, and not an exhaustive review of the many battles that occurred in Norway during the short two-month military phase of the war. However, to provide a context for a reader to understand the stress and anxiety endured by families living during an overpowering invasion, with a near certain outcome of defeat, I want to review one additional very critical battle – the struggle by Allied forces from Britain, France and Poland to retake Narvik from German control. The failure of the Allied military effort in central and southern Norway, and the cancellation of the effort to retake Trondheim without question were catastrophic setbacks. The British Prime Minister Neville Chamberlain still held out hopes that Narvik could be retaken from the Germans. The Allies believed that if the Germans could be blocked from access to Narvik (and iron ore from Sweden) they would not be able to wage a war beyond a few months. 2

In the last chapter we saw that the British had gained a potential upper hand for the retaking of Narvik by a stunning Naval victory, in which over a three-day period they had sunk all ten German destroyers in the vicinity of Narvik. The Germans at Narvik, rather than consolidating their military position, were busy rescuing and treating the 2,500 survivors of their naval disaster, and burying hundreds of their dead comrades.

Expecting to take advantage of the British naval victory, on April 14, Admiral of the Fleet Lord Cork, aboard the cruiser *Aurora*, sent the following message to General Mackesy:

In view of successful naval action at Narvik yesterday, 13th April, and as enemy appear thoroughly frightened, suggest we take every advantage of this before enemy has recovered. If you concur and subject to information we shall receive tonight, 14th April, from Warspite, I should be most willing to land military force at Narvik at daylight tomorrow, Monday, from Aurora and destroyers. Supporting fire could be provided by cruisers and destroyers. And I could assist with a naval and marine landing party of 200 if you wish. 3

General Mackesy was totally unprepared for such a quick action. He had already set up camp at Haarstad, a Norwegian fishing town on an island about 50 miles northwest of Narvik. In addition he had landed some of his troops 140 miles north of Narvik, and another contingent of troops about 35 miles north of Narvik. He thought in terms of unopposed landings of troops, rather than landing troops where Germans could attack. Furthermore, his troops had neither snow shoes nor skis and many had never seen a mountain before and certainly not mountains with permanent snow fields and glaciers. 4 (Narvik is at a latitude further north than Nome, Alaska).

On April 18, Lord Cork met with General Mackesy at the base at Harstad to discuss the retaking of Narvik and to try to settle their differences. General Mackesy was adamant in expressing his desire to be cautious. He said:

It is not a justifiable operation of war for a numerically inferior force, scarcely able to move owing to the snow, to attack an enemy who enjoys all the advantages of the defensive. When the difficulties of landing from open boats on very limited beaches are added, the operation becomes sheer bloody murder. 5

The two commanders sent word to London that evening. Realizing the widely different views on how to attack the Germans at Narvik, Winston Churchill responded by transferring the command of all forces in the Narvik area to Lord Cork. Admiral Cork then engaged in a personal reconnaissance of the Narvik Beaches. He found it impossible to move more than a few feet; with snow up to his waist, travel even short distances was exhausting. 6

How vulnerable were the German forces in Narvik after the British navy sank all ten German destroyers at Narvik? The situation was so grim that the Fuhrer was contemplating that General Dietl and his forces at Narvik evacuate and cross the border into Sweden. On April 17 Hitler actually gave such an order for immediate transmission to General Dietl instructing him to evacuate Narvik. The order was held up temporarily by Lieutenant-Colonel von Lossberg, and shortly thereafter German intelligence obtained information that British commanders were vacillating and were not prepared to launch an immediate invasion of Narvik. After receiving the surprising news that Britain was unprepared for an immediate counter attack, Hitler rescinded the order to retreat and instructed Dietl to hang on as long as possible. 7

Admiral Cork decided on a plan to use his force of one battleship, two cruisers and eight destroyers to shell Narvik, hoping that the German defenders of Narvik would raise a white flag. On April 24 his ships initiated a three-hour bombardment of Narvik in a blinding snowstorm. The snow storm was such that the crew of the British naval ships could not see the destruction done by their barrage, nor any sign of a "white flag." The operation was aborted. The advantage that the British had after the destruction of the German fleet at Narvik and the chaos that followed as Germans rescued survivors and buried dead, was now gone. The German defensive position at Narvik was consolidated and included the addition of the 2,500 Germans who survived the sinking of their fleet.

Assault on Narvik Halts as Neville Chamberlain Reconsiders the Disaster and Resigns

As stated in the previous chapter, on April 26 Chamberlain decided to withdraw forces from central and southern Norway. The allied invasion had gone very badly. The swift German advance throughout key areas of Norway, combined with powerful air attacks and the destruction of ports, made it impossible for the British to land heavy military equipment, or even to land substantial numbers of British and allied forces. The Allied forces that were landed were not equipped for the winter and snow conditions they encountered, causing many soldiers to suffer from hypothermia and frostbite. Indecision by the British was certainly a major factor that led up to the crisis that was now viewed as beyond repair. For example, even on April 9, the day of the German invasion, the British believed that the major port city of Trondheim should be attacked by the British navy and then held by army and marines. Although the plan was developed at a preliminary stage at that time, it was cancelled, then reconsidered, cancelled again and reconsidered again before being finally cancelled on April 26 because Trondheim was, by late April, a German fortress. In the midst of all this, several Norwegian cities (Namsos, Aandalsnes, Molde and Kristiansund) were utterly destroyed by near round-the-clock raids by German bombers. 8

The political uproar in Britain, caused by the complete collapse of the British and allied forces in Norway, led to a non-confidence vote for Prime Minister Neville Chamberlain. Knowing that he could no longer govern, he arranged to meet on May 9 with Lord Halifax and Winston Churchill. He told the two of them he could no longer govern, and asked them who he should recommend that the King of England appoint as the next Prime Minister. After a long pause of sustained silence during which neither Lord Halifax nor Winston Churchill said a word, Lord Halifax finally spoke at length, but said in effect, 'not me.' Chamberlain arranged to meet with the King of England to recommend Winston Churchill as the next Prime Minister. 9

May 10, 1940

The morning of May 10 came the news that German forces had attacked Holland and the Netherlands with overpowering force and speed. Amidst news that all of Europe was about to be engulfed in a conflagration, the King of England called Winston Churchill to Buckingham Palace, where the King asked him to form a new government and to serve as the Prime Minister.

The Battle for Narvik continues

As the Allied forces prepared for a final attack to gain control of the important port city of Narvik with its vast railway capability, problems were apparent. On the one hand they did have a total of more than 30,000 troops well equipped with anti-aircraft guns, air support, tanks, and a very large British Naval force including troop carriers and landing craft. In addition the French General, Antoine Marie Bethouart, was experienced in mountain warfare and thus a good choice to lead French and Polish forces in the upcoming attack. But there were problems. The crack French troops arrived without skis and snowshoes, and the Polish troops had never seen a mountain and were untrained to fight in mountainous conditions. This lack of preparation for the conditions that existed at Narvik caused British, French and Polish troops to suffer from frostbite and hypothermia. The 3,500 Norwegian troops were well prepared for the weather and terrain and excelled in cross country ski travel. However, the Norwegians troops were short of ammunition. An additional problem was continued disagreements among the Generals about how to proceed. General Mackesy persisted in calling for a slow and cautious approach to capture Narvik. 10

The three Generals, Lord Cook of the British Admiralty, General Mackesy and the French General Bethouart finally agreed to defer an immediate attack on Narvik, and first occupy the Oyord Peninsula by attacking the port and fishing villages of Bjerkvik, Meby and Ojord.

The attack on German positions at Bjerkvik began after midnight on May 13, with a massive naval bombardment by the British fleet consisting of the battleship *Resolution,* the cruisers *Effingham* and *Vindictive* and five other destroyers. Assured that the civilian population had been evacuated, the protracted naval barrage began, followed by the unloading of tanks and troops. The Germans were well dug in and also equipped with machine guns. As the battle progressed the town of Bjerkvik was destroyed and in flames. The Norwegian civilian population had not been warned of the attack and had not evacuated; many women, children and old men were killed. 11 However, the German forces were defeated. At this point the cautious General Mackesy was removed from his command and replaced by General Claude Auchinleck. 12 Soon the combined allied forces also gained control of the Norwegian towns of Meby and Elvegaardsmoen after heavy fighting, and then proceeded to attack and capture Oyord.

On May 27 the German Luftwaffe destroyed the port city of Bodo to hamper British military movements. At 11:45 p.m. Narvik was bombarded by a massive British naval attack as the much delayed and anticipated attack to capture Narvik finally began. Narvik with its large port, its vast railroad lines and terminal, its homes and churches was destroyed in the effort to take it from the Germans. By the end of May 28, Narvik (in ruins) was in Allied hands. 13

The same day (May 28) the British, French and Polish troops prepared to evacuate Narvik and all of Norway. The Norwegian General Ruge and his 3,500 troops who fought with the Allied forces to retake Narvik were not told of the allied plans to evacuate all of Norway and leave it to the Germans. General Fleischer, the Norwegian Commander in Chief, had not been informed, and neither had King Haakon nor members of the Norwegian government.

On May 30 the British General Auchinleck wrote a letter of protest about the secrecy of keeping from the Norwegians what was about to happen to their country. He wrote the following to General Ironside:

The worst of it all is the need for lying to all and sundry in order to preserve secrecy. Situation vis-à-vis the Norwegians is particularly difficult, and one feels a most despicable creature in pretending that we are going on fighting when we are going to quit at once. 14

The next day (May 31) the War Cabinet again decided to postpone the decision of whether or not to inform the Norwegian government and its Generals of the Allied plans to evacuate all forces from Norway and leave the country to the Germans. General Auchinleck and Lord Cork decided on their own to disobey orders. They traveled to Tromso and met with Sir Cecil Dormer who agreed to meet with the Norwegian government and inform them of the plan to evacuate all forces from Norway. The Norwegian Defense Minister Ljungberg asked if the Allied forces could leave behind weapons and supplies so the Norwegians could continue the struggle. The answer was no, that is, "Everything must be taken away." 15

After hearing this very disturbing news, King Haakon, Prince Olav and members of the Norwegian government considered their options during this terrible and conflicted time. Eventually, they decided they could serve their country best by continuing to provide leadership from England. However, General Ruge insisted that he would remain in Norway and be with his troops when they laid down their arms to the Germans.

At eight o'clock on the evening of June 7, 1940, the British cruiser *Devonshire* hoisted anchor and sailed for England, with the Norwegian government and King on board. 16

On June 9, General Ruge gave the order to his troops to disband the Norwegian 6th Division. The Norwegian military campaign had ended, but Norway had not surrendered.

The German Military Victory in Norway: What was Accomplished?

1. Once Germany repaired the Narvik harbor and the rail lines connecting the Port at Narvik to Swedish iron ore mines, Germany was able to receive an uninterrupted supply of iron ore throughout the war. The amount of iron ore amounted to 600,000 tons in 1941, 1.8 million tons in 1943, and remained high into the year 1945.

2. Germany gained strategically important naval and air bases in Norway that were positioned east and north-east of the British Isles. The long and deep fjords in Norway and the high mountains provided unexcelled cover and protection for the Germans. From these bases Germany could attack the convoys in the North Atlantic that were vital to supply the British. Similarly, the bases in Norway enabled German air and naval forces to attack convoys travelling from the U.S., Canada and Britain to the Russian port of Murmansk. Note: The German victory in

Norway came at one cost that later proved very serious for the Germans. Germany lost a large portion (one half) of their surface naval ships. Later in the war when allied convoys sailed to the Russian port of Murmansk to aid the Russians in their fight against the German invasion, the German naval losses caused an initial delay in their efforts to disrupt convoys in Arctic waters.

The Spectre of Defeat of Allied forces in Norway: The situation in England

The defeat of the Allied forces in Norway resulted in a change of government in England. Neville Chamberlain left office early in May 1940, and Winston Churchill took over as Prime Minister. Winston Churchill was better suited than Chamberlain for handling the grave peril that was shortly to confront England, all of Europe – and the world.

The Spectre of Military defeat for Norwegians

Norwegians were to learn what they were made of as they faced an occupation by a Nazi government following the defeat which ended the military phase of the conflict.

Norwegians faced the presence of between 350,000 to 500,000 German troops for the remainder of the war. In effect there was one German soldier for every eight Norwegians. Against such overwhelming force the Norwegians developed a powerful resistance movement that the German occupying forces were unable to defeat.

The German occupying force itself had undergone an abrupt change even during the short two-month military conflict. The German diplomat Kurt Brauer was summarily removed from his position by Adolph Hitler. Brauer had made two mistakes: First, he failed to get one of two outcomes from the Norwegian King Haakon, i.e., his agreement to surrender or his capture. Secondly, Brauer failed to establish a Norwegian Administrative Council that would agree to work in collaboration with and under the control of the Nazi occupying force. Brauer had met a number of times with three Norwegian leaders: Chief Justice Paal Berg, Governor I.E.Christensen and Bishop Eyvind Berggrav. The three Norwegians never agreed to the formation of a government council that would usurp the official Norwegian government and collaborate with the German occupying forces. Hitler appointed Joseph Terboven to take direct administrative control of occupied Norway on April 20, 1940.

Chapter 4

LIFE AND FAMILY PROBLEMS FOR US IN NAZI-OCCUPIED NORWAY

My parents faced two immediate problems that created extreme stress for them as their beloved country was now occupied by the feared Nazi-regime. My father received a notice that his two-year visa to travel to Norway was about to expire and he would lose his U.S. citizenship if he did not return to the United States. In addition, my mother was pregnant and was expecting the birth of her third child sometime in mid to late August 1940. Both my mother and father thought it would be unfortunate for him to lose his citizenship. They both knew that my mother could not risk taking the long trip to the U.S. during war time, when she was so close to giving birth. As the military phase of the war ended June 7, 1940, my parents worried about these family issues in addition to the travails brought on by the defeat of Norwegian and Allied forces and the occupation of Norway.

My father was able to get in contact with the American Consular office in Bergen, and he asked for an extension due to the war. The answer was negative. He was told that if an opportunity to leave came, he must do so or lose his citizenship. In July 1940 notice came that the United States was sending a ship, the *American Legion,* to Petsamo, Finland, to pick up American citizens in now war-torn Europe. My parents discussed the option and each agreed that my father should go on the *American Legion* and the two boys (Roy and Leif) would stay with their mother in Norway. It was a heart-wrenching decision, but neither ever challenged the other about the choice. My father left in mid-July and traveled first to Olso and then through Sweden and on up to Petsamo, Finland. He boarded the ship with about a thousand other American citizens. On August 16 at 2:00 a.m. the ship left the dock to travel across the most northern tip of Sweden and Norway down the North sea, through a passage between the Shetland Islands and the North of Scotland to the Atlantic Ocean and continued on its way to New York City.

Three days later back in Rubestadneset, Norway, Roy and I were playing in the front yard. My mother was talking with her mother-in-law who had just brought over some berries from her garden. Then we heard an airplane and the terrific noise of the airplane's engine as the plane gained speed as it also came closer and closer to its target near us. The plane dove close to the ground and the engine roar reached a peak and then the plane dropped bombs that exploded nearby with a tremendous shattering noise. Roy and I ran for the house, and Roy said to me we must get to the basement. I still remember clearly how afraid I was of the bombing but I was also afraid of running down the steep stairs to the basement. Roy grabbed me and carried me down the stairs. I would not have made it in one piece otherwise. I was two years and eight months old. That memory is my earliest memory of anything, and I can still recall it vividly. The bombing raid also served as a marker for me and I then began paying attention, even as a very young child, to news and experiences about the war and the occupation.

Five days later, on August 24 my mother gave birth to her third son, John Edward. Because of the war, my mother did not have the option of going to a hospital to deliver her child. The baby was delivered with the help of a local, trained midwife. A few days later my mother began to go through a depressive episode. She described it as follows:

* * * * *

The enemy occupation, Alf's departure, the bombing of our village and the recent birth of a baby all began to have their effect both on my physical condition and mental attitude. Everything seemed so hopeless. I was convinced that no happy future was in store for us, and my tor-

mented mind told me I would never again see my husband. I ate and slept little, and I became physically weak. After putting the children to bed, I sat in the kitchen and cried, night after night. In the children's presence I acted cheerful, and I tried never to let anyone know how hopeless everything seemed to me.[1]

War and occupation incidents increased and added to my early memories. I am still disturbed by the memory of seeing German soldiers marching past our house with rifles and military vehicles and knowing that my mother was outraged by their presence. One day, when I was about 31/2 years old, as I was alone playing in our front yard, I paused to watch about twenty soldiers march past carrying weapons. I picked up a stone and threw it at them. I later told my mother. She scolded me severely. Also, German soldiers searched our house. The intrusion of German soldiers in our house upset and angered my mother.

There were also some happy events during this period, unrelated to the war. My paternal grandmother lived nearby and I visited her every day. She was a favorite. Like grandmothers everywhere she loved being around grandchildren and gave me undivided attention. She often made Norwegian pancakes out of potato flour, from an old folk recipe. When served warm, right off the wood burning stove with a little bit of butter and sugar, it was perfect. When I was with her, time stood still. She was never in a hurry, and she liked to tell stories or listen to anything I wanted to say. She was like this with all her grandchildren. Her daughter, my father's sister Alma, and her husband lived nearby with their seven children. Grandmother had no favorites; we were all special to her. These extended family contacts created a sense of security and support during the time of the hated occupation.

I was not aware of hunger or of our family being short of food and basic essentials. But, as was the case for all Norwegian families during the occupation, food was strictly rationed in amounts less than adequate. My mother, like other parents, fed her children what we needed first before she ate. I was too young to understand that food shortages were part and parcel of living in an occupied country during war. Mom also spent much time making clothing for her children, sewn from pieces of cloth cut out from clothes my father had left behind.

Fear and Dread During the Nazi-Occupation

As a young child, I was aware of and anxious about what I could understand of the war and the occupation, namely:

1. German soldiers marching in front of our house,
2. German soldiers searching our house,
3. The fright of the bombing raid.

My mother was concerned about the above three problems, but much more concerned about issues that I was too young to understand. They include the following:

4. Norwegian leaders were required to sign an oath of support of the Nazi – occupation of Norway, including Lutheran ministers, school teachers, physicians and health care workers, and members of trade organizations.
5. All Norwegians were required to turn in radios (except the minority of Norwegians who supported Quisling – and Hitler). The penalty for violation was death.
6. Norwegians were required to identify Jews, and were forbidden to assist them.
7. Contact with the enemy (England) was punishable by death. This included efforts to escape to England.
8. The small percentage of Norwegians (fewer than three percent) who supported Quisling, created very serious problems. For example, members of a group called "Hirds" who supported Hitler were encouraged and given authority to commit acts of violence with impunity, against the majority of Norwegians who resisted the occupation.
9. Unlike my limited perspective as a four-year-old, my mother was aware of the vastly bigger picture of the war engulfing the world. WW II started with the Nazi invasion of

Poland in 1939, then Norway and Denmark in April 1940, later France and all of Europe including Russia, then other continents such as Africa and Asia. The rapid spread of the war and the possibility of a Nazi victory created intense fear – but also an absolute resolve to resist.

These intrusive demands explain why German soldiers had come into our house to search. They were looking to see if my parents were hiding weapons, radios, or people such as resistance fighters or Jews. As a young child I did not understand why armed German soldiers had come into our house to search and to question my mother. My parents, like all Norwegian citizens, were under pressure to forego their personal, religious and cultural freedoms and values and accommodate and comply with an oppressive occupation. It was unacceptable to them. When my mother was handling this alone without her husband, she wanted very badly to escape the Nazi occupation. In Norway as in all countries embroiled during WW II, unarmed citizens suffered more casualties and encountered more hardships than members of the armed forces of the nations who were fighting the war.

The next two chapters will review how the Norwegian Church responded to the Nazi-occupation (Chapter Five), and how the schools and other professional and trade groups reacted to the Nazi-occupation (Chapter Six).

Chapter 5

THE CHURCH RESPONDS

Church leaders provided an early and broad-based resistance in Norway during the occupation. Their resistance drew upon the information about previous tactics used by Nazi forces in Germany. For example, Ronald Fangen, a well known Norwegian Christian author, had visited Germany in the 1930's and wrote about the Nazi suppression of Christian leaders in Germany who opposed the Nazi regime. He wrote about the Nazi suppression of the Confessional Church and the imprisonment of Pastor Martin Niemoller. Concern about the expected effort by Nazi authorities to muffle and weaken the effectiveness of the Church in Norway led Church leaders to meet on October 28, 1940, to form the Christian Council for Joint Deliberations. 1 This group, including all seven Bishops in Norway, was determined to speak out fearlessly against Nazi intrusion into Norwegian values and culture. The group pledged to speak with a unified voice and to ignore clerical divisions. Church leaders did not restrict their opposition to matters that solely pertained to traditional church functions, but broadened their opposition to include the Nazi use of violence and intimidation and its disregard for traditional laws that protect rights of citizens.

Church leaders noted with great concern a pattern of violence used by Nazi authorities in an effort to bludgeon submission from Norwegians. For example, on November 30, 1940, a band of young Quisling storm troopers entered a classroom of the Oslo School of Business, attacked and badly beat up the instructor and some students. 2 At about the same time another group of Quisling storm troopers (called Hirds) entered the headquarters of the Trondheim Student Association and asked the chairman of the association to put up a placard in support of the Quisling party. The chairman, Mr. Holterman, refused and was beaten. 3 These attacks and others were done with the approval of the Nazi occupation forces in Norway. On December 14, a Nazi official issued a decree instructing the police to give 'active support' to the storm troopers (the Hirds), and warned that refusal to support them would be looked upon as an action 'inimical to the state' and would give rise to severe punishment. 4 The Hird groups consisted of young men who were recruited by Nazi officials and instructed in the use of violence and intimidation to suppress opposition. From one locale to another throughout Norway, the Nazi- organized Hird Jamborees entertained young recruits and spread Nazi propaganda about the "new order,' and espoused anti-Semitism.

The Nazi occupation forces maneuvered to establish complete control of law and order. To accomplish this, on November 14, 1940, the newly formed Nazi Department of Justice announced that the Nazi regime had the sole authority to dismiss and to appoint judges, jurymen and mediators to handle trials and prosecutions in Norway. 5 This meant that any action (however violent) taken by pro-Nazi forces would receive legal sanction.

Another major concern during the Fall of 1940 was the newly published order that the long established oath of silence of clergy was abolished. 6 Under this new ruling, a police officer could ask a clergyman to give names of church members who opposed the Nazi-occupation, or the names of Jewish church members who had converted to Christianity. Refusal meant the threat of imprisonment for the clergyman.

In November 1940 Ronald Fangen, the Norwegian author who wrote about Nazi suppression of Church leaders who opposed the Hitler regime, was arrested and imprisoned. 7 This news caused a sensation throughout Norway, but did not deter the readiness of Church officials to remain focused and vigilant.

Bishop Berggrav Portrayed as Pro-Nazi

The Nazi occupation forces wanted as little trouble as possible from the Norwegians. One approach was to publicize names of prominent Norwegians who supported the Nazi occupation forces. A few weeks after the military defeat of forces in Norway, the Nazi-controlled Norwegian press and radio announced that the highly regarded Bishop Berggrav supported the Nazi occupation. Posters were circulated throughout Norway which stated: **"Let us follow our leaders, Quisling, Hamsun and Berggrav."** [8] Quisling was a traitor who supported Hitler. Hamsun was a famous Norwegian author, who was pro-Nazi. I would liken him to Charles Lindberg, who also supported the Nazi movement in the United States. However, Bishop Berggrav never supported the Nazi occupation forces, and he was among the strongest voices among Norwegian clergy against the social injustices brought on by the Nazi occupation forces in Norway. It took a substantial effort by Bishop Berggrav to undo the damage by the false reports and to convince Norwegians that he had not been consulted about his name being used by the Nazi occupation forces and to restate his strong opposition to the Nazi occupation of Norway. One outcome of the scandalous use of Bishop Berggrav's name was that Norwegians eventually stopped listening to Nazi-controlled Norwegian radio. Norwegians, like my parents, listened only to BBC broadcasts.

The Church Makes Strategic Actions

On January 15, 1941, the Norwegian Church leaders sent a letter to the Nazi Minister of Church and Education, Rognar Stancke. The letter was signed by all seven bishops of Norway, including Bishop Berggrav. The long letter focused on the foremost problems encountered by Norwegians as a consequence of the Nazi-occupation forces during the early phase of the German occupation of Norway. The concerns were the following:

1. The violence by the Hird group against law-abiding Norwegians in an effort to intimidate Norwegians who opposed the Nazi occupation;
2. The action of the Nazi-occupation forces to dismiss at will

all legitimate members of the legal courts of Norway and to replace them with pro-Nazi members, and:

3. The Nazi ruling to abolish the clerical oath of silence, which was an attack at the very heart of the Church.

When Minister Skancke failed to respond, three of the bishops – Berggrav, Scoren, and Maroni – with the approval of the other bishops arranged an interview with Skancke to reiterate the concerns and to emphasize the serious nature of the issues. In their communication with Skancke, they gave a blunt warning:

The Church is not interfering in worldly affairs when it exhorts the authorities to be obedient to the highest authority which is God. When the leaders of the community permit violence and practice injustice and coerce the soul, then the Church is the guardian of the soul. 9

Three days later Ragnar Skancke responded urging the ministers of the Church to act in the spirit of good will and to support the "new order." Stancke reiterated the new requirement that the clerical oath of silence had been revoked.

The Church leaders responded by issuing a pastoral letter explaining the whole affair and made it known to every congregation in Norway. 10 This Church action received immediate positive response from individuals and groups throughout Norway. On February 14 Skancke issued a warning that such pastoral letters were illegal and could not be read to congregations. Church leaders ignored the prohibition. In many cases throughout Norway military police attended church services prepared to arrest a minister who read a "pastoral letter." Not yielding to pressure, the church also had the pastoral letter printed and 50,000 copies were spread all over the country. The police raided the major printing companies in Oslo on February 17, 1941, in order to find the printers responsible. The printing press was "underground' and not discovered. 11

In March 1941 Ragnar Skancke issued a decree that all religious broadcasts on radio must be approved by Propaganda Chief

Gulbrand Lunde's Department of Culture. This was to ensure that Christian broadcasts in Norway were written in the "New Spirit."

All Christian radio broadcasts in Norway ended. No clergy permitted their service to be censored by a Nazi-group. Throughout Norway the Nazi-controlled "Norwegian State Broadcasting" was shunned. Norwegians listened to Norwegian language broadcasts from London and other free broadcasts. 12

Synagogue in Trondheim Is Desecrated and Confiscated

The Nazi relentless abuse and oppression continued. In April 1941 the Synagogue in Trondheim was taken over by German troops and vandalized. Chandeliers and religious objects became targets for pistol shootings. The Synagogue then became a housing center for German soldiers. Jewish citizens were arrested, beaten and imprisoned in the Vollan prison in Trondheim. The assaults in Trondheim were directed by Ernst Flesch, a Gestapo commander. Under his directive four Jews were shot to death – they had listened to the forbidden BBC Broadcast and passed on information to others. 13

Members of the Jewish community met with the Protestant minister who later became Bishop Arne Fjellbu. After reviewing the concerns and the oppression of the Jewish community in Trondheim, Arne Fjellbu arranged a meeting with the Nazi mayor Olav Bergan and the Nazi District Governor Frederik Prytz. Accompanying Fjellbu was the dismissed former District Governor Johan Cappelen (he had been dismissed because he was not pro-Nazi). They explained to the Nazi officials that it would be a shame if Trondheim should be the vanguard of Jewish persecution in Norway. The Nazi officials warned Fjellbu that the Church would be threatened if the clergy were to be outspoken. Fjellbu answered that it would be even more dangerous for the Church to maintain silence. 14 At this period in 1941, Nazi oppression of Jews in Norway was severe but localized and targeted. Later the Nazi oppression of Norwegian Jews escalated to a maximum level.

The Common Prayer and Paper Clips: Threats to the Nazi New Order

For hundreds of years part of each church service in Norway would include a "Common Prayer." Within the prayer were some brief lines asking God to support the King, his family and the Norwegian government. After the Nazi forces occupied Norway, the Norwegian Bishops were informed that the prayer must be changed. The King and the "old Norwegian government" were not to be included in the prayer because they had been replaced by the Nazi forces and the New Order. The prayer instead must ask God to bless the Nazi governance of Norway. Bishop Berggrav said, "No!" The Germans initially insisted, but a compromise was reached. The Clergymen agreed not to recite the name of the King, his family and the Norwegian government in exile. The Nazis withdrew the requirement that the prayer include a plea to God to support the Nazi governance of Norway. During subsequent church services, the minister recited the prayer and paused at the point of mention of the King and the government of Norway. At that moment the congregation in unison (without instruction) recited the now forbidden words of the prayer as before. In no Christian Church was there a spoken prayer to ask God to bless Quisling and the Nazi occupation of Norway. [15]

Norwegians in very large numbers used a barely noticeable symbol to indicate support of the King and the traditional governance of Norway. The symbol was a simple paper clip attached to a shirt pocket or jacket. It meant, "We must stick together." Even this was seen as a threat by the Nazis, and occasionally a Norwegian wearing such a paper clip could be attacked or arrested. [16]

German Forces Invade Russia

German forces invaded Russia on June 22, 1941. This major development in the war caused profound changes in the entire warfront. It meant, for example, that Great Britain would not be faced with an imminent threat of an invasion of German troops. Russia became one of the allied forces and in a year's time received huge amounts of aid in the form of military equipment shipped from England and the U.S. and Canada across the Atlantic and up the coast of Norway and on to Russian ports, such as Murmansk on the Barents Sea. In Norway the Nazi regime enforced efforts to use Norwegian labor and factories to produce war materials for the German effort in the war against the Russians. The Nazis put tremendous pressure on Norwegian clergy to endorse publicly the German invasion of Russia.

German officials in Norway apparently expected that Norwegian Church leaders would make an announcement to the Norwegian people in support of the German invasion of Russia because the Russians were "Godless." They assumed that if major leaders in Norway would show support to the Nazis their governance of Norway would be easier.

Of the one thousand clergy in Norway, a very small number did support the Nazi movement. In all twenty-seven quislings among the Norwegian clergy prepared and signed a text that supported the German invasion of Russia. Their text was the following:

The final, decisive battle against Bolshevism and the international godlessness movement is now in progress. Everyone must realize now what is at stake. On it depends whether our children shall continue to have a Christian upbringing and a Christian school. On it depends how far we shall continue to retain the Christian faith, morality and culture in this land.

The undersigned pastors call on the Norwegian people to stand together during this fateful period for our land and people.

For Norway and Finland against Bolshevism. 17

(Signed by 27 clergymen)

In late July 1941 the seven bishops met to review critical issues facing the church in Nazi-occupied Norway. Following the meeting, Bishop Berggrav was asked by the editor of a Nazi publication what decisions the Clergymen had made regarding the fight of the German military against the "Godless Bolsheviks, that is the Russians." The editor had written an article trying to convince Norwegians that good Christians should appreciate the military attack on Russia. In his article he asked for a response by the Norwegian clergy. In response to the editor of *Fritt Folk,* Bishop Berggrav replied:

"The war-political question which you discuss in your article, has not been made an issue at the episcopal meeting and naturally was not among the matters discussed." 18

The refusal of the bishops to give support to the German invasion of Russia, brought on serious and protracted threats to Church leaders in Norway. It was the beginning of a new phase in the struggle of the church in Nazi-occupied Norway. The quisling newspaper *Fritt Folk* and *Hirdmannen* published statements including the following: *"...those clerics who do not do the natural duty of every Christian by supporting the fight for the existence of Christianity, they are not Christians, but hypocrites who misuse the Christian name and the ministry for the sake of the salary."* 19

Norwegian Clergy Required to Sign an Oath in Support of Nazi Occupation

On September 11, 1941, the Nazi-controlled Department of Church and Education sent a letter to all the country's clergy and asked them to sign a statement indicating their support of the Nazi occupation. If they could not support the Nazi occupation, they were to give their reason and sign it. Church leaders responded that the request was illegal, and would be ignored. 20

February 1, 1942 Quisling Proclaimed "Minister-President:" Churches across Norway Are Shut Down

On February 1, 1942, Terboven appointed Quisling as Minister-President of Norway at a carefully orchestrated ceremony at the ancient fortress of Akershus in Oslo. Quisling was determined to bring Norwegians in line with the Nazi forces in Norway. He would require the church leaders to support the Nazi-program, and he would require all teachers, health care workers and laborers to support the "new order." 21 While Quisling was being proclaimed as "Minister-President," military police blocked the doors of the Nidaris Cathedral in Trondheim. That was the first Norwegian Church to be shut down during the occupation. 22 When pressed further to support the Nazi-occupation of Norway, all seven bishops resigned on February 22. Several church leaders were arrested, including Bishop Berggrav. Of 854 ordained clergy in Norway, almost all resigned and their churches were shut down for the duration of the Nazi-occupation. The church continued as a "free church" but could not use the church buildings, and the ministers received no salary. The few churches that remained open were referred to by Norwegians as "Nazi-churches." These few "Nazi-churches" were led by clergy who supported the Nazi vision of the new order. 23

Church Reaction to Extermination of Jews

Minister President Quisling announced October 27, 1942, that all property belonging to Jews was to be confiscated and all Jewish men over 15 years of age were to be arrested. 24 By the time of this announcement the Nazis had a complete list of all Norwegian Jews, including detailed information about their personal data, work history, wealth, family and social connections. Furthermore, Jews had begun to be arrested in large numbers after 6.00 a.m. the day before.

Sixty clergy who formed the Temporary Church Leadership Group protested. The following is a portion of a long letter sent to Minister President Quisling and read throughout Norway in informal church assemblies:

For 91 years Jews had a legal right to reside and earn a livelihood in our country. Now, they are being deprived of their property without warning, and thereafter the men are being arrested and thus prevented from providing for their propertyless wives and children. This conflicts

*not only with the Christian commandment of "love thy neighbor,"
but with the most elemental of legal rights. These Jews have not been
charged with any transgressions of the country's laws, and much less
convicted of such transgressions by judicial procedure. Nevertheless,
they are being punished as severely as the worst criminals are punished.
They are being punished because of their racial background, wholly and
solely because they are Jews.*

*This disaffirmation by the authorities of the Jew's worth as human
beings is in sharp conflict with the Word of God which from cover to
cover proclaims all racial groups to be of one blood. See particularly Acts
17:26. There are few points where God's Word speaks more plainly than
here. God does not differentiate among people. Romans 2:11. There is
neither Jew nor Greek. Galatians 3:28. There is no difference. Romans
3:22.* 25

The ministers, without access to their pulpits, urged Norwegians to resist collaboration with the Nazis and to support their
Jewish neighbors.

The Nazi Strategy to Persecute Norwegian Jews

Oskar Mendelsohn has contributed information to the Resistance
Museum in Oslo, Norway and has written the book: *The
Persecution of the Norwegian Jews in WW II.* The following is a
summary of the escalation of severe oppressive actions taken by
the Nazi occupation forces in Norway against Jews.

The first action against the Jews by the German occupation
force was to get a list of all Jews in Norway. German officials
contacted the major Synagogue in Trondheim and the one in
Oslo, in May 1941, explaining that Jews were free to worship,
but that the occupation force required a complete list of the
membership. Police districts, which eventually came under the
control of the Nazi occupation, were given the responsibility to
compile complete lists within their district, along with information about Jewish owned companies, real estate and membership
in organizations. By 1942 the occupation force knew the names

and addresses of every Jew in Norway, each of whom carried an identification card with the letter "J" stamped on it. 26

Then Jews were required to turn in all radios. This preceded the requirement, later introduced in September 1941, that all Norwegians, except pro-Nazi Norwegians, were to turn in radios. 27

Anti-Semitic articles and posters were widely distributed throughout Norway. Some of the propaganda drew upon historical facts about a period of time in Norway when anti-Semitism was extensive. For example, the Norwegian Constitution, written in 1814, had a paragraph which explicitly stated that Jews were not to have the possibility of citizenship in Norway. 28 During that period the only religion that could be practiced in Norway was worship in the State Lutheran Church. Even Christian denominations other than Lutheran were not permitted in Norway. In 1841, the law was amended to give Norwegians the right of freedom of religion. However, that did not apply to Jewish worship. The law was amended again in 1851, giving Jews the option of Norwegian citizenship and freedom to practice their religion without prejudice. That change was due largely to the effective influence of the Norwegian author Henrik Wergeland. 29 The Nazi propaganda tried to influence Norwegians to go back to the time of the early 19ᵗʰ century, when anti-Semitism was the norm in Norway. The propaganda was not effective, in large part because of the strong opposition to anti-Semitism by the Norwegian protestant clergy and other leaders including the Norwegian government in exile.

Another Nazi-propaganda effort was the widespread publication of quotations from Martin Luther's pamphlet: "Von den Juden und ihen Lugen." (The Jews and their Lies). This extremely anti-Semitic piece of writing was used by the Nazis to espouse their racial views. However, Norwegian clergy had already spread the word that Martin Luther's anti-Semitism did not reflect Christian values. 30

In April 1941, German troops confiscated the Synagogue

in Trondheim and executed a number of Jews and arrested and imprisoned others (see section above).

In June 1941, Ragnar Skanke, the Norwegian pro-Nazi appointed as head of Church Ministry, attempted to institute a policy that citizens applying for a marriage certificate must produce evidence that their parents and grandparents were not of Jewish origin. Bishop Berggrav replied on behalf of all the bishops that the recommendation was against Christian values and would not be supported. Implementation of this policy was delayed until after the churches were shut down in early 1942. [31]

In September 1941, the Protestant clergy were required to sign a statement supporting the Nazi occupation including the Nazi racist policy. As stated above this attempt failed.

In the fall of 1941, Minister of Justice Sverre Riisnaes began to implement a legal basis to ban Jews from the ownership of real estate. [32]

1942 In Memoriam

In January 1942, at the Wannsee-conference in Berlin, the Germans decided "the final solution to the Jewish question" for all the occupied countries. The Jews were to be deported to extermination camps on the continent, especially Auschwitz in Poland. [33]

The exact words of the "Law" dealing with the arrest of Jews and the confiscation of Jewish property came by telegram to all police stations in Norway on Sunday October 25. The content is as follows:

All male persons above the age of 15 whose identity-card bears a "J" shall be arrested regardless of adult age and be transported to Kirkeveien 23, Oslo. The arrest shall be made on Monday, October 26 at 6.00 a.m. The prisoners shall bring cutlery, ration-cards and all identity documents. All property is to be confiscated. Attention is to be made to all bonds, stocks and shares, jewelry and cash. Such items are to be actively searched for. Bank-accounts are to be blocked and safety deposit boxes shall be emptied. Confiscated objects shall remain with the police until further notice. Registration documents shall immediately be sent to this office. Administrators must at once take over the management of the enterprises of the arrested. Records of the arrested stating citizenship, in particular for earlier German citizens, are to be sent to this office. All adult female Jews are given daily obligation to report at the office of the criminal department of the ordinary police. 34

Chief of State Police

Starting in the morning of October 26, Jews were arrested and transferred from areas throughout Norway to a large prison camp at Berg outside of Tonsberg. The barracks at the camp lacked bunk beds, bedding, tables, chairs and kitchen utensils. Bathroom facilities were not available; temporary latrines were long logs. The barracks were unheated. As the flood of prisoners arrived they were told that to attempt escape meant execution followed by the execution of ten fellow prisoners. 35

One month after the beginning of the mass arrests, on the evening of November 25, the prisoners were taken to the Oslo harbor. At the Oslo harbor they joined other prisoners, including women and children, and boarded the huge vessel, the *s/s Donau*. On this first trip to concentration camps on the continent 532 Norwegian Jews were on board. The ship reached Stettin before noon on November 30, and the prisoners boarded a train for Auschwitz. The historian Oskar Mendelsohn writes that documents still exist confirming the delivery to Auschwitz which reads: "The taking over of 532 Jews from Norway is hereby acknowledged". 36

In all a total of 760 individuals were deported from Norway identified as Jews by the Germans. Most met death at the gas chambers. Only 25 survived; they were rescued when the Russian army liberated Auschwitz in late January 1945. 37

The names of the victims are engraved in memorials erected in cemeteries in Trondheim and in Oslo.

Escape to Sweden

When Germany began to deport Norwegian Jews to death camps in Germany, Sweden made an offer to German officials to provide refuge for Norwegian Jews. Sweden had reason to believe that since Germany was totally dependent on Swedish steel they might have made an accommodation to their ruthless policy of extermination. German officials absolutely refused. In Sweden, as in Norway, Church leaders and members of other organizations were outspoken in their rage about the persecution of Jews. In response to the failed effort to sway German officials, members of a Swedish resistance group joined with members of the Norwegian resistance movement to assist Jews to escape to Sweden. This was a very high risk enterprise. If they were caught, the Germans killed both the Jews and the persons who were assisting them. This happened a number of times. Some Norwegians committed suicide when capture was imminent. However, a total of 925 Jews managed to escape to Sweden with the assistance of members of Norwegian and Swedish resistance groups. 38

Chapter 6

SCHOOL TEACHERS AND PROFESSIONAL AND TRADE GROUPS REJECT NAZI DEMANDS

In the last chapter we saw the church stand firm against the Nazi demand that the clergy sign an oath of support for the Nazi occupation of Norway. Had the clergy signed the oath, they would have consented to such requirements as to modify prayers during church services to ask God to bless the Nazi occupation forces in Norway, to agree to Nazi censorship of Christian broadcasts and to endorse the Nazi racist policy (anti-Semitism). The clergy were not alone by any means in having to either comply (i.e., collaborate), or face potentially severe consequences for refusing Nazi demands.

It is worth reviewing select segments of the speech given by Vidkum Quisling on the evening of the dreadful day of the invasion, April 9, 1940.

Fellow Norwegians. ... The German government have (sic) offered their assistance to the government of Norway, together with the solemn assurances that our national independence would be respected. ... Under present circumstances, all resistance is not only senseless, but also criminal, for it imperils the life and property of our fellow countrymen. All civil servants, all municipal employees ... are duty-bound to obey orders of the new government. Any failure to do so would expose the transgressor to the full rigors of justice. 1

In November 1940 each of 14,000 teachers in Norway received an order from Ragnar Skancke (head of the Department for Church and Education). The order required each teacher to sign an individual declaration of loyalty to the Nazi regime and express his/her willingness to "work positively and actively to promote my pupils' understanding of the new ideology and view of society as stated in the program of 'Nasjonal Samling,' (NS) and for the actions and decisions of our new national government." 2

A member of the teaching profession sought guidance from Bishop Berggrav. Bishop Berggrav drafted a counter-declaration that was reviewed by education leaders from many sections of Norway and by Judge Ferdinand Schjelderup, a distinguished member of the Supreme Court. A copy was then sent to all teachers in Norway. The text is as follows:

> *With reference to the enquiry received, I hereby declare that I will remain true to my teaching vocation and my conscience, and that on that basis I shall, in the future as in the past, carry out the decisions relating to my work which are lawfully given by my superiors.* 3

More than 12,000 of the 14,000 teachers, in protest, signed the counter-declaration and returned it to the Nazi leadership in Norway. This created a crisis because the occupation forces did not expect that the vast majority of teachers would reject their demands. In response the Nazis unleashed other assaults against teachers, students and their parents. Those teachers who did not withdraw their protests would lose their jobs. In addition, teen age and young adult members of the Hird organization perpetrated violent attacks against teachers and students, and destroyed school property. 4 The Hird gangs were started by Quisling and modeled after similar Nazi programs in Germany. Quisling named the gangs after a tradition of pagan Viking kings, a thousand years earlier, who had employed rough and tough body guards named Hirds with sworn loyalty to the Viking rulers. As stated in previous chapters, the Hird groups had protection from Nazi-controlled police organizations throughout Norway. Many Norwegian children showed opposition to the occupation forces by wearing a paper clip conveying a subtle symbol meaning: "We must stick together in support of our King and in opposition to the Quislings." Other children wore a patch on their clothing symbolic of King Haakon VII.5 These symbols often provoked fights with Hird members. In February 1941 violence initiated by Hird members was so disruptive that school teachers and students went on strike. Also in February 1941, authorities required school children in Oslo to attend a Hitler Youth Exhibition. The request was followed by widespread demonstrations by students and parents. School authorities told the NS representatives they would NOT comply. The demand was finally dropped.6 Since youth members of a Hird group were in the minority, they were often attacked as well.

The vast majority of Norwegians ostracized the minority (less than 2 percent) of the population who supported Quisling. The treatment in Norway was known as the "ice treatment."7 Known Quisling supporters were isolated and shunned. Children of Quisling supporters were socially isolated, even by relatives. Parents of a youth member of a Hird group were similarly ostracized. One can imagine the level of stress that these factors introduced to the school classroom environment.

In mid February 1942 the Nazi-controlled Ministry of Education issued a statement requiring the teachers to withdraw their protest (the counter-declaration), and sign the oath of allegiance to the "new order." Those who refused would lose their jobs by March 1. Essentially no teacher withdrew his/her refusal to support the Nazi regime. The Ministry declared the schools closed for the month of March1942. On March 20, 1942, one teacher in ten (about 1,300) of the dissenters were arrested and sent to concentration camps. Most of them were sent to the furthest north concentration camp in the world, a place called Kirkeness in far north Norway – at a latitude comparable to Pt. Barrow, Alaska. 8 These teachers (now prisoners) were subjected to torture and hard physical labor. The dissenting teachers who were not arrested were in no way different from the ten percent who were arrested. The Nazi occupation regime apparently felt they could not put all the teachers in concentration camps, so by the end of March1942 the remaining resisters were permitted to teach and the schools were reopened.

Farmers Guild is Briefly Nazified

Early in the Autumn of 1940 the Farmers Union (Norges Rondelag) was pressed to be part of the "new era" and merge with the NS Guild of Farmers. The chairman of the Farmers Guild, Johan Mellbye opposed any collaboration with Quisling and the Nazi occupation forces. In response, Mellbye and the general secretary of the Farmers' Union were removed from office by the Nazi commissary minister in the Department of Agriculture. This action placed the Farmers' Union under Nazi control.

Within days of this development an unsigned circular was sent to farmers throughout Norway giving detailed information about the action taken against the Chairman of the organization and what led to it. A copy was sent to London and Norwegians heard the BBC broadcast in its entirety.

The message was as follows:

The Union of Norwegian Farmers has ceased to be a free organization for the protection of the farmers' needs; it has become the instrument of Quisling's interests. Every farmer in Norway must see to it that this instrument is knocked out of the tyrant's hands. There is only one way of doing this: by resigning from what was formerly the Union of Norwegian Farmers. Rally round your old chief, the former Cabinet Minister Mellbye. He and his life-work are in danger, but you and you alone can save both him and it by lining up firmly with him against those who imperil the Norwegian cause. You now possess the power in the land, nobody can govern today against the farmers' will! Let Minister Mellbye's urgent appeal to the district chairmen find a response in every honest farmer in Norway. Let us hold together, let us show strength. 9

The appeal worked. The Nazified Union became a paper organization supported exclusively by a handful of farmers who were pro-Quisling. The Gestapo tried in vain to discover the source of the unsigned circular. The source was Tore Gjelsvik, who was an expert in agriculture and a leader in the resistance movement in Norway. He survived the war undetected.

Ship Owners Reject Nazi Demands

At the start of the war Norway had the fourth largest merchant marine fleet in the world. The Norwegian merchant fleet had more freighters and oil tankers than either Germany or Japan. Gaining these ships and their experienced crew would have been a major advantage for the Nazi war effort. Having heard at sea of the invasion of Norway, the captains did not return to Norway; instead they headed for English ports. In the summer of 1940 each ship owner in Norway received a Nazi demand to broadcast orders to their captains to return to Norway. This order was refused. Instead, every ship owner ordered their captains to travel to English ports When that transfer was accomplished, over one thousand Norwegian freighters and oil tankers and their crews were employed in the vital North Atlantic convoy service, shipping military equipment such as airplanes, tanks, jeeps, trucks and ammunition to England from Canada and the United States. The Norwegian freighters also shipped large amounts of military supplies to Russia after Russia was brutally attacked by Germany. One of the Norwegian freighters active in the North Atlantic convoy system was the *SS Brant County*; our family escaped on this ship as it left London on January 5, 1942 as part of a convoy of 40 ships. The resistance by the ship owners meant arrest, and internment in prisons in Germany for refusing to turn over their ships to the Nazi war effort. 10

Representatives of 43 National Organizations Speak Out

In February 1941 the Nasjonal Samling (NS) issued a proclamation that all appointments to professional, labor, education and church positions had to be approved by a newly formed NS Personnel Office for the Public Service. The NS Office went on to remove from office several well known and respected civil servants who did not fit in with the "new order." In Oslo a leading physician was removed from his position at the Oslo municipal hospital and arrested. In response all the doctors at that hospital resigned as did other senior doctors at other Norwegian hospitals. The NS was forced to retreat and the doctor was released from prison and returned to his position.

These events led key individuals in all professional and trade groups throughout Norway to communicate among themselves and to prepare a broad - based protest. On May 15, 1941, the chairmen of forty-three national organizations prepared a letter of protest, signed it and sent it to Josef Terboven (Reichskommissar). The document took the offensive and protested a full range of illegal demands and violent actions by the Nazi occupation forces in Norway, and called on Josef Terboven to account. The letter ended thus:

Accompanied by threats or other forms of pressure, a demand to join the (NS) Party or to work actively for the advance of the Party represents for the overwhelming majority of Norwegians a deliberate attempt to induce them to compromise with their consciences and depart from what they consider right and proper.

It is plainly evident that among our people everywhere this has led to a growth of disquiet, which greatly impedes ordinary daily work and so damages the country. The disquiet and irritation have lately approximated to a state of embitterment.

We venture to request the Reichskommissar urgently for a reply, to be given at the earliest possible moment, to the letter of 3 April as well as to the present application. 11

Before considering the response by Josef Terboven to the protest letter he received and signed by representatives of 43 national organizations, it is worth reviewing the ongoing Nazi warnings to Norwegians. In mid-December 1940 A.V. Hagelin, as Acting-Minister for Home Affairs, re-issued a notice demanding that public servants should give positive and active support for the NS and the "new order." "Failure in any degree will be treated as action against the State, to be visited with drastic penalties." 12

On June 18, 1941, Josef Terboven summoned the representatives of the 43 organizations to a meeting in the parliament building in Oslo and made a furious speech condemning the group. Five of the signatories were arrested on the spot. Some of the organizations were dissolved by Terboven, and in the others the leaders were dismissed and replaced by individuals known to be supportive of NS. 13

Quisling's Return to Power: Act one, the Ungdomsfylking Law

Vidkun Quisling had pronounced himself the head of Norway the evening of the April 9, 1940, German invasion. Within a week Kurt Brauer had convinced Adolph Hitler that the Norwegians might accept the German occupation, but not Quisling. Quisling was removed from a position of power and Josef Terboven was placed in charge of the occupation of Norway. Joseph Terboven, who perhaps had a short memory, appointed Quisling to the office of "Minister-President" on February 6, 1942. This occurred after Quisling made promises to Nazi authorities that he could bring the Norwegian populace in line with Nazi ideals. On February 6, 1942, Quisling decreed the Ungdomsfylking Law which stipulated that all children between the ages 10 and 18 years must become members of the newly formed Nazi youth organization and do "service." The youth would also be indoctrinated in Nazi values and ideals. 14

Families across Norway were deeply distressed. The Norwegian clergy, still disturbed by the Nazi takeover of the Nidarus Cathedral in Trondheim on February 1, met to discuss the Nazi assault on families with this new law pronounced by Quisling. All seven bishops met in Oslo on February 14, 1942, and prepared a protest letter to Ragnar Skancke, the NS Minister of Church and Education.

The first half of the bishops' response to Ragnar Skancke stressed the idea of the importance of the parents in raising their children and providing a Christian and moral education. The letter pointed out that parents have full responsibility for how they permit others, including schools, to participate in the forming of children's character and ideas. The final portion of the response to the NS Minister of Church and Education is the following:

A good home's inner freedom has always been a foundation pillar in our society and no one can by force break into a home and create antagonism between parents and children without God's commandment being trampled under foot.

In all this the church and the parents stand inseparably bound by their conscience and by God's command. He who would attempt to force the children out of the parents' bonds of responsibility and to disrupt the Divine right of the home, would at the same time be forcing the parents to the utmost act of conscience.

Every father and mother knows that they one time will stand answerable to the Almighty for how they have brought up or let others bring up their children. Here they must obey God more than man.

As the overseers of the Church, we recognize it as our duty to present this clearly and unmistakably upon the occasion of your having received orders to assist in the formation of a law aimed to compulsorily mobilize all children from the age of 9-10 years and upwards to an influence which countless parents must recognize as intolerable in relation to their conscientious obligations.

An intrusion of this kind will touch the people in their innermost and deepest life. To those who in their conscientious distress have turned to us in this matter we have for the present not been able to give any other answer than that we have sent you this remonstration. A copy of it is being sent simultaneously to Minister Axel Stang. 15

The letter was signed by the seven bishops: Eivind Berggrav, J. Storen, J. Maroni, Andreas Fleischer, Gabriel Skagestad, Henrik Hille, and Wollert Krohn-Hansen.

Minister Skancke replied to the bishop's letter by attempting to justify the government's position based on a tradition of Christian support of obedience to civil authority. Skancke specifically referred to writings of Martin Luther who supported obedience to government rulers. Skancke also referred to the "New Order" and to a vague danger of Norwegian people "plunging over the precipice." He ended his response to the bishop's letter as follows:

The State was ordained by God just as much as the family and just as much the Church. The Church has no right to interfere with the State's right and duty to endeavor, on the basis of this, its responsibility, to solve its educational problem with regard to the people.

The State's view, then, is briefly this: If the Norwegian people are to be saved from plunging over the precipice, then the children must be saved.

If our Norwegian people are tomorrow to become a strong and healthy people who understand their times and will the good, then the children must learn to understand their times and will the good. It is for this that the Nasjonal Samling's Ungdomsfylking, with the National Youth Leader at the head, wants to educate the Norwegian children.

To call this compulsory mobilization only goes to show how little the Church's bishops themselves understand of the New Order. Now for once it is impossible to shut oneself out from the ground-breaking time of a people. It must inevitably result eventually in one's having shut himself out from the people themselves and in being left behind. 16

The message from Skancke was clear. He would not compromise with the *Ungdomsfylking law, which* obligated all Norwegian children between the ages of 10 and 18 to be involved in NS programs of indoctrination and service. Within a short time after the protest letter against the law affecting children, Bishop Berggrav was captured and placed in a concentration camp. Bishop Wollert Krohn-Hansen, and 45 pastors were also arrested. In addition, all of the seven bishops were dismissed by Quisling and Skancke.

Minister-President Quisling then appointed seven individuals who were members of Nasjonal Samling to be the new bishops of the State Lutheran Church of Norway. After Easter Sunday in April, 1942, all the clergy of Norwegian Churches in Norway resigned their posts. They were free from NS influence, but also lost salary and access to church buildings. As stated above the handful of churches that remained open were referred to by Norwegians as "Nazi churches" and they were shunned. 17

As to the Ungdomsfylking law. Norwegian parents showed resistance by ignoring the requirement.

End of Part I. It is my hope that the brief chapters in this section have given a sense of the dread faced by Norwegians during the Nazi occupation. The reasons were sufficient to convince my mother that she should risk the hazards of escape and refugee status to escape the Nazi occupation. The next section of this book was written by my mother, Harriet Terdal, and entitled: Our Escape from Nazi Occupied Norway.

PART II

OUR ESCAPE FROM NAZI-OCCUPIED NORWAY

HARRIET TERDAL

WRITTEN 1971

Chapter 7

APRIL 9, 1940

We were awakened in the early morning of April 9, 1940, by airplanes flying low and circling around our little community located on the island Bomlo, off the western coast of Norway.

For several days we had heard rumors about the German fleet in the North Sea, but few believed anyone would invade the neutral, peace-loving Norway; however, the planes we saw were German. Soon we learned that the Germans had indeed invaded Norway. Although unprepared, the Norwegians fought and many died for their country. England and France sent troops who landed and fought at several parts of Norway, but soon had to retreat. The Germans were too powerful and after a few weeks had taken over the country.

Living in an enemy-occupied country can never be fully understood if not experienced. The Nazis' initial step was to seize the newspapers and the radio stations, and from then on we were fed their lies and distorted truths.

My husband, Alf, our two small sons, Roy, almost five years old, and Leif, six months old, and I had returned to Norway from the United States in the summer of 1938, planning to stay for awhile or perhaps settle.

Just prior to the invasion, Alf had a notice from the American Consular office in Bergen that his visa, valid for two years, was about to expire. He had gone to the office and applied for an extension; meanwhile the Nazi invasion and occupation took place. For awhile we had no communication with the outside world, but when these restrictions were lifted, the answer from Washington came, and it was negative; if an opportunity to leave came, Alf must do so or lose his citizenship. No ships from the outside world entered the ports of Norway, however, knowing that they would be confiscated by the Nazis and put in their service.

Living a rather secluded life in a small village, Rubbestadneset, located on an island, we didn't get any Nazis in our community right away, but we certainly felt their presence in the country. Food was rationed immediately. Every week new rules and regulations were published and always with threats of severe punishment for violators. Blackouts were at once enforced. No lights were to be seen after dark. Since it was now summer, and the days were long, that proved no immediate problem.

When the British and the French troops had to withdraw, the situation grew worse, for the Norwegians seemed to have no hope of getting rid of the enemy.

An encouraging note was that the king and the royal family had been able to escape. King Haakon was safely in England after a dangerous and strenuous flight. Crown Prince Olav and Crown Princess Martha and their three children were safe in Sweden. It also gave us great satisfaction to know that the national gold reserve had been safely moved from Norway to England.

We were not allowed to display pictures of the Royal Family in our homes. When an act is forbidden, it becomes precious. Never before had the Royal Family meant so much to the Norwegian people. They stood for freedom, love, peace, harmony, and understanding.

Since the main industry in Rubbestadneset was a diesel motor factory, which was also equipped with slips for repairing the many fishing vessels which came there, soon the German ships found their way to Rubbestadneset for repair. Many of these German ships had been seized from Norwegians. When a man lost his boat, which was his means of making a living as a fishermen, there wasn't much left for him to do. Whenever Nazi ships were being repaired at Rubbestadneset, the crew swarmed all over the village. In the stores they bought the choicest of everything. Then they would march in our street, singing songs about their inevitable victory, a prospect which further depressed us.

We canceled the subscriptions to the newspapers, as they were Nazi- controlled and thus unreliable sources of information. We still had our radios, but didn't listen to the Nazi-controlled radio stations in Norway. Instead we were able to get news from England, both on the English broadcast and from the Norwegians who had set up a government in exile in London and broadcasted regularly. Of course, the news from London wasn't too encouraging either, but at least we listened to friends, not enemies.

*　*　*　*　*

When open warfare had ended in Norway, bold and fearless men and women went underground and continued working for their beloved homeland. When caught, they were mercilessly tortured and imprisoned in concentration camps or were executed. A deep fear overwhelmed us with the mere mention of the word, Gestapo. Soon young and older people escaped to England, many out of fear of the Gestapo, but the majority to join the Norwegian Government in exile and vol- unteer for any service where they could be of most help. Many joined the merchant marines; others went into training in the military either in England or in Little Norway, Toronto, Canada, to be prepared for services in the Norwegian airforce. Many were schooled in espionage and secretly returned to Norway. Others were trained for the extremely dangerous task of keeping illegal traffic open between Norway and England or the Shetland Islands, or making commando raids at strategic points on the long coast of Norway.

*　*　*　*　*

In July an announcement came over the radio that the United States was sending a ship to Petsamo, Finland, to pick up American citizens in now war-torn Europe. Alf got in touch with the American Consular office in Bergen which gave him instructions on how to proceed. We spent a few hectic days preparing him for departure and trying to get permission for me to go along. At that time I was not an American citizen. We had some influential friends in Oslo who interceded for me at the American Embassy there, but to no avail. Roy and Leif were born in the United States, but it seemed wisest to keep them with me. It was impossible for me to take a chance and travel to Oslo with Alf and plead my own case at the Embassy, for I was pregnant and soon expected a baby.

Alf was hesitant about leaving us, but I felt he shouldn't risk losing his citizenship. I tried to appear calm during this time, but when he finally departed and I was alone with the children in an enemy-occupied country, I was heartbroken. I kept hoping that another ship would arrive on which the children and I could travel to the United States. Now all-out war was raging in Europe, and the Nazis showed no mercy.

I received a note from Alf from Oslo, then one from Sweden, but no more. These were tense days, full of anxiety and uncertainty. Finally we heard via radio that United States citizens from all over Europe had reached Petsamo, Finland, where they were to embark on s/s *American Legion*. Then we heard the ship had departed from Petsamo and was on its way across the Atlantic. It was now August.. We learned that President Roosevelt had invited Crown Princess Martha and her children to be the guests of the United States for the duration of the war.

On Sunday, August 18, with my thoughts mostly on the ship and Alf, I became worried lest Hitler would harm it because of the Royal Family onboard. Late that evening it became evident that I had cause for alarm, when the news came over the radio that Hitler had threatened the ship. He wanted the *American Legion* to take a different course than the one President Roosevelt had decided upon. The President refused to take orders from Hitler and followed the original route. I continued to worry about Alf's safety.

I Give Birth, Bombs Fall, Alf Has Departed

Monday, August 19, was a beautiful, clear day. Because it rained almost the year around at Rubbestadneset, a clear sunny day was always a welcome sight. I didn't feel too well and thought that would be the birth day of my third child. In spite of intermittent pain, I was busy getting everything in order before my confinement. In the afternoon, about 4 p.m., my mother-in-law visited me bringing berries from her garden. The children were outside playing, but Roy had just come in complaining that he didn't feel too well. He was running a temperature and lay down.

Suddenly we heard an airplane and a terrific noise. We ran to the window and saw the plane dropping bombs—several of them. The noise was shattering. The plane flew away and it was quiet. My first thought was that there would be many dead or wounded. We were later told that only one person, a young man, had been hit by shrapnel. Again hearing the sound of a plane, we were certain that it had returned to drop more bombs and ran down into the cellar for coverage. Later we learned that it was a German ambulance plane coming to take the wounded man to the hospital in Haugesund. He died enroute.

Although shocked, we felt that our little village had been miraculously spared from many casualties. The plane that had dropped the bombs was British, who had been erroneously informed that German soldiers were stationed at the schoolhouse. Thus the target had been the school, which was extensively damaged. Usually on a nice day children would romp about on the school playground, but on that day not one child was playing there. The custodian had finished cleaning the building, and was on her way home when the bombs fell. Although shrapnel penetrated some homes, no one was hit except that one man.

As for Roy and myself, his fever disappeared in the shock and excitement, so did my pains.

Hearing the noise from the bombs, the midwife, living about seven miles away, had immediately become concerned about me, knowing I expected my baby any day, and she came as fast as she was able on her bike. The midwife then insisted the boys and I come to her house and stay, along with the Feroy family, who lived upstairs; they were her personal friends. We got a ride with Alf's cousin, Benjamin, who with his family also evacuated. All the people who had someone to whom they could go left Rubbestadneset. The general feeling was that the first bombing had been a warning, and the next target would be the factory, since it was most useful for the Germans in getting their ships repaired.

The midwife wanted the children and me to stay in her home until the baby was born, but I felt it was better for Roy and Leif to be in their own home in familiar surroundings. The Feroys continued to go to her home and sleep for several nights.

Because our house was on the outskirts of the village, Alf's mother slept in our spare room. Another family, whose home was near the school and factory, asked if they might use our finished room in the basement; they lived there for several weeks.

On Saturday morning, August 24, Edward was born. Because of the war and Alf not being home, I preferred not to leave the children to go to the nearest hospital, in Bergen. And so I was confined at home with the assistance of a midwife and a trained baby nurse.

The happiness which usually follows the arrival of a newborn child was overshadowed by the constant reminder that we were no longer a free people, but overtaken and dominated by a brutal and unscrupulous foreign power. I did feel greatly relieved, however, when the news came that the ship, *American Legion*, with Alf onboard, had safely arrived in New York.

*   *   *   *   *

The enemy occupation, Alf's departure, the bombing of our village and the recent birth of a baby all began to have their effect both on my physical condition and mental attitude. Everything seemed so hopeless. I was convinced that no happy future was in store for us, and my tormented mind told me I would never again see my husband. I ate and slept little, and I became physically weak. After putting the children to bed, I sat in the kitchen and cried, night after night. In the children's presence I acted cheerful, and tried never to let anyone know how hopeless everything seemed to me.

Then one night while lying awake in mental anguish, I suddenly realized that this indulgence in self pity had to stop. I scolded myself: "You should be ashamed for feeling so sorry for yourself. Pull yourself together; you have three children who are depending on you." Then I thought of the many things that, after all, I ought to be thankful for. For instance, I knew my husband was safe in the United States, while so many women were unaware whether their loved ones at sea were dead or alive. I had a home that had not been taken away from me by the occupational troops, nor bombed, and I had three lovely children. Also we did have food even if we couldn't get everything we were used to.

So that night I started to count my blessings, realizing I had so much to be thankful for. And I believed in God, and could take my problems to Him in prayer. Victory over despondency and worry wasn't won overnight, but as time passed, when I woke during the dark hours and worry and anxiety started to flood my brain, I was gradually able to push them into the background by dwelling on our many good things. During that difficult period of my life, I learned to count my blessings and thank God for all the good things He bestowed upon me from day to day.

*   *   *   *   *

My widowed mother, together with her brother, lived in Arendal in the southern part of Norway. Since the invasion on April 9, and during the summer, my mother had never mentioned the Germans in her letters. We had to be careful what we wrote, never knowing if our letters would be censored, but the fact that mother didn't even mention the Nazis' presence worried me. I thought maybe she was too scared. Although still clinging to a hope of a ship that would take the children and me to the United States, I definitely couldn't leave without knowing how my mother and uncle were. I couldn't phone them because the phones were tapped.

In October I hired a woman to stay with the children so I could take the trip to Arendal and find out how they were. A journey that usually took one day now took two because of travel restrictions and reduced transportation facilities. I left Rubbestadneset early in the morning of October 16, traveling by ferry and bus to Haugesund, where I boarded a steamer for Stavanger. At Stavanger I got a train for Flekkefjord. It was close to midnight before the train arrived there. I was told by other passengers that the bus to Arendal wouldn't leave before the next morning. Having never been to Flekkefjord before, I asked a lady sitting next to me on the train about lodging for the night. Other travelers heard my question and began to inform me about the situation. Grand Hotel, they said, was taken over by the German officers, but the Bondeheimen had no Germans because that hotel was more or less reserved for the farmers when they brought their products to the city. I asked how I could find Bondeheimen. This was midnight, and with blackouts strictly enforced, it was pitch dark. A salesman told me he was going there for the night also and I could accompany him. Now this was something I would never normally have considered, but this was no ordinary circumstance. I was grateful to walk with him to the hotel where I got a small room on the first floor.

The next morning I boarded the bus, changed bus in Kristandsand and late that afternoon arrived in Arendal.

I was greatly relieved to discover that my mother and uncle accepted the situation rather calmly. Because Arendal is a coastal city thousands of occupational troops were stationed at various strategic points. My mother and uncle, however, living in the country in a secluded spot away from the main thoroughfare, didn't see much of them. Since this was in the early stages of the occupation, they could still get reasonably good food—but by the time the war was over, my mother and her brother were down to less than half of their normal weight.

Assured that my relatives were as safe as anyone could be under the dreadful circumstances, and concerned about my children, whom I missed desperately, I stayed only three days before beginning the long, tedious return trip to Rubbestadneset.

The first day I got only as far as Kristiansand, about 60 miles, where no bus left for Flekkefjord until the next morning. I got a room in a hotel, swarming with Germans. Taking a little walk in the city, I noticed large signs above several stores, stating that each was a Jewish-owned store, and not to patronize it. The Nazis carried on their persecution of the Jews also in the countries they had seized.

The next morning I boarded the bus, arrived in Flekkefjord in the afternoon and got a train to Stavanger. When I arrived in Stavanger late that evening, with the blackouts strictly enforced, it was again pitch dark. The boat I was going to take to Haugesund didn't leave before the next morning, so once again I had to get lodging for the night.

I'd heard about the Mission Hotel not too far from the railroad station, asked for directions and proceeded to find it in the darkness in unfamiliar surroundings. I had a flashlight, but once I was stopped by a policeman and warned to be careful in my use of it. I finally arrived at the hotel only to be informed it was filled to capacity. I saw many German officers in the lobby. The night clerk phoned to different hotels for me but none had a vacancy.

"What shall I do?" I asked, "I can't walk the streets all night."

His answer was unsympathetic; "You don't have to walk the streets; you can always go to the police station." He failed to tell me, however, how a stranger could find it in the darkness of the night. Due to the gasoline shortage, no taxis were available. My only hope was that the ship I was going to take to Haugesund the next morning had arrived and I could stay on it overnight. Asking directions, I finally got to the pier and there was the boat! It was a great relief to get onboard and get a cabin for the night.

The next morning the ship left Stavanger and about noon arrived in Haugesund. Here I had to wait for a bus to take me to Forde, and there I got a ferry to Rubbestadneset. I arrived home late at night, tired, but happy to be home and find that my children were all fine.

I had been warned before leaving on the trip to be extremely careful in speaking to strangers about the war and the Germans, a person would never know who might be spying for the enemy. But people spoke quite freely, I discovered, about their disgust and anger over the audacity of the Nazis to seize a neutral country, and to make the inhabitants obedient by exercising cruel and harsh rules, with severe punishment for disobedience.

*　*　*　*　*

The Norwegian government had stored a large supply of food because of the unsettled condition in Europe. But the supply dwindled quickly with the many Nazis stationed in the country. When the war hit Norway, people stocked up so much on clothes, yard goods and shoes, that many had a good supply for some time. But soon after the occupation, everything was rationed—food, clothing, fuel. We had stamps to use when shopping, but even with the stamps, the stores had little to offer, and provisions were difficult to obtain. It became commonplace to walk or bicycle four or five miles just to get a pound of oatmeal, a little butter or a few eggs. Because my mother-in-law had a cow, I was able to get a quart of milk from her every day for Edward, the baby. Once in a while I was lucky to get a couple more quarts from a neighboring farm.

I had not bought extra clothing when war came hoping to be able to return to the United States. By and by the children's clothes started to wear out. Roy, the oldest, especially needed clothes; the other two could use hand-me-downs. By then, however, little or nothing in the clothing line was left to purchase.

I knew a seamstress, Ingborg Folgroy, trained in sewing both women's and men's clothing. Her husband was also in the United States, while she and her small daughter remained in Norway. Fortunately, she was able to help me make over some clothes for the children. Ingborg came to my house during the day and sewed and went home each evening. She skillfully made over Alf's old pants and overcoat to fit Roy. We made two old navy blue wool flannel bath robes into long pants for Leif, and both pants and jacket for Edward.

One day while sewing, Ingborg said: "Do you plan to escape: is that why you are having these clothes made over for the children?" I said no, the children needed the clothes, but as we continued talking about the depressing situation in Norway, and our husbands so far away, our conversation centered about ways of leaving the country. We had heard of people traveling through Sweden, Russia, Siberia and Japan to the United States. Realizing it would be difficult to make such a trip, which would require permission from the German officials to leave the country, after much discussion we decided to try. First, we had to travel to Bergen to talk with the German officer in charge.

Living on an island, quite a distance from Bergen, it was necessary for us to travel by a small passenger and cargo ship. The trip took almost the whole night with several stops along the way. The ship had no passenger cabins, so we sat or partly reclined on hard wooden benches in the ladies lounge. Ingborg and I were the only passengers that night. No food was available on the boat.

I Seek Permission From A Nazi To Leave Norway

In the early morning upon arrival in Bergen, we soon found a restaurant and had breakfast. Although dreading the trip to the German office, that was our reason for being in Bergen, so we put on our bold faces and determinedly strode towards the building and went in.

A young Norwegian Nazi was at the reception desk.

"What do you want?" he asked.

"We would like to speak to the officer in charge."

"About what?"

"To ask permission to leave the country and travel to the United States."

He became furious, stamped his feet on the floor, swung his arms and screamed,

"Why do you want to leave Norway?"

I answered: "Our husbands are there and we want to be united with them."

Telling him about the whole disgusting situation in Norway we didn't dare.

"The officer is busy now. You'll have to wait here." And with that he pushed us into a large size closet with no windows; a small light dangling from the ceiling revealed a couple of chairs. Weak with fright we dropped down on them.

Ingborg said: "We will never get out of here alive!"

"Of course we will," I said, attempting to reassure her, but I wasn't too hopeful myself, wondering what would happen next.

Finally, after what seemed an endless time, he came back, opened the door and grudgingly announced, "The officer will see you now."

After the encounter with the young Norwegian Nazi, we didn't know what to expect from the German, and we were quite scared. To our surprise and relief, however, he was quite pleasant. The officer greeted us and asked, "What can I do for you ladies?"

I responded, "We are here to ask permission to leave the country and travel via Russia to the United States where our husbands are."

In poor Norwegian mixed with German he replied, "When you have all your travel arrangements in order, I'll give you permission to leave."

"Will you give us a statement in writing now?" I asked.

"Certainly," he replied and wrote on a sheet of paper that when an opportunity arrived for us to leave, we had permission to do so, and signed it. Was he a kind man or did he suspect that our plans wouldn't materialize? I'll never know.

Happy with this accomplishment, we went to the American Consular Office and told the Counsel about our plans. We showed him the written permission to leave the country
by the German officer.

"This looks authentic enough," the Consul commented.

"My three boys are American citizens; will you kindly help me with a passport for them?" I asked.

"Yes," he answered. "First, you have to get passport pictures and mail them to me. Then I shall make out the passport."

The day's events had been so exciting and successful beyond our hopes that we ignored our feelings of hunger and fatigue. My companion and I returned to the dock where the boat was anchored and spent the night returning home.

Soon we started the preliminaries for getting our passports. Ingborg Folgroy and her daughter got their Norwegian passports in order. I procured an American passport for my three small sons and a Norwegian passport for myself. But before we could start to apply for visas to travel through Sweden, Russia and Siberia to Japan, and from there to the United States, war broke out between Germany and Russia, closing that door of travel for us. Although it then seemed that all our efforts had been for nothing, the passports I had acquired for the children and myself became extremely useful later on.

*   *   *   *   *

It was now summer, 1941, and the Nazis had been in Norway for more than a year. As they experienced tough resistance from the Norwegian people, the Germans became increasingly ruthless and austere with their resistors. It's difficult to understand how so-called civilized people could resort to such inhuman tortures on a people who only tried to free their country from oppression. With fear and anger we heard about the tortures in the concentration camps, the deportation of prisoners to Germany, and the many who were executed. (In every little community in Norway is a monument with the names inscribed of those who gave their lives for their country.)

We had been able to listen to news on our radios and in that manner keep up with happenings both in Norway as well as the outside world. But in August a proclamation went out that all radios must be turned in, time and place designated. Failure to comply—death. People who had more than one radio, however, kept one, hid it and kept listening to news from England in spite of the threatened severe punishment. The Stavland family, who lived upstairs in my house, kept one radio, and I went there off and on and listened to the news. I had the advantage of understanding English.

Mr. Stavland worked in the office at the factory. One morning he returned home, pale faced. He told his wife and me that Gestapo was just about to land on a boat, and rumors were that they came to search homes for illegal possession of radios. Mr. Stavland took his radio, hid it in the woods and said that if he got away with it this time, he would never listen to it again. The Gestapo didn't stop and search homes on Ruabbestadneset that time, however, as they went farther out on the island for their searching; and we continued to listen to the news.

* * * * *

Our food rations became smaller and smaller and of poorer quality. Bread has always been an important part of the Norwegian diet. By early September the bread we got was dark brown in color and doughy as it couldn't be baked properly. For that reason we weren't allowed to eat it the day it was baked—nor could we have been able to either. The bread was better when it was a week old and had dried. Even then it tasted awful. We didn't know what we were eating because unrecognizable ingredients had been added to the flour to make it go further.

My first reaction was that I couldn't possibly feed it to the children, but soon realized I should be thankful to have it to give to them. Since I had three small children with food stamps for all of them, we didn't starve, but the nutritional value of the food was insufficient.

* * * * *

By early October we again heard rumors that the Gestapo were on the way. Nothing good ever came out of a visit by the Gestapo. Some men from the underground had committed an act of sabotage and then escaped. Now the Gestapo were after them. The Germans were coming to Bremnes as it was the most likely place for the fugitives to hide until they could get a boat and escape to England. The Gestapo men were also going to search for radios and other objects that we weren't allowed to have.

The Gestapo Search Our House

On Sunday morning, October 12, my nephew Leif Helland, delivered a quart of milk which Grandma Terdal so generously allotted me every day for my children. Leif was excited and burst out: "The Gestapo have arrived; there were some at home when I left!" Roy and Leif had gone to Sunday school; I was home alone with fourteen-month-old Edward.

Before long there was a knock on the door. Opening it, I saw three young Nazis. When they learned that a family lived upstairs, two of them went there, and one came into my apartment. He walked around from room to room and asked questions. He was friendly, but I was weak with fright and upset about the intrusion, so I was rather curt in my replies.

"You look angry," he remarked. "Why?"

"That's the way I always look," I answered.

I wanted to ask him how he would have acted if someone had occupied his country by force, and then had the audacity to enter his home uninvited. But that would have been sufficient cause to throw me into prison.

"Where is your husband?" he asked.

"In the United States," I replied.

He didn't seem to believe me; probably he thought that Alf was a saboteur, too, and had escaped to England.

"Do you get letters from him?"

"Yes."

"May I see one?"

By then I was quite provoked. I picked up the letter that had arrived the previous day and dropped it on the table.

"Here it is," I said, "but do my letters have to be censored twice?"

He looked at the envelope and the U.S. stamps on it. "I don't have to read it," was all he said.

Although I resented the intrusion, when upon learning later how they'd gone about in other homes, opening drawers and searching closets, I was grateful to have been spared that nuisance.

The Gestapo went from house to house looking for the fugitives and illegal possessions, but with no success. When they gave up their search and returned to Bergen, the fugitives came out of hiding, and were assisted in their escape to England.

* * * * *

When the door to travel from Norway to the United States via Russia was closed, I thought of the many who managed to escape Norway. Some fled to Sweden, but the great majority crossed the North Sea over to England. As we lived on Bremnes, on the western coast of the country, getting to England seemed the least difficult for myself and the children.

Even though the coast was heavily patrolled by the Germans, its rugged coastline and many little islands made escaping comparatively easy. At least twice a week a little boat would leave Bremnes for England. Hundreds of small fishing vessels secretly left the enemy-occupied homeland and set out for England.

I had discussed with my mother-in-law the possibility of escaping, and she thought we could make it safely to England. I wouldn't have considered doing this without her knowledge and consent, but I told no one else of my plans.

One of our friends, Ola Olsen, was busily involved in the

underground movement. Risking his own life, he helped countless people flee to England. Many of them were being pursued by the Gestapo because of their resistance to the Nazi regime and their homefront activities. One day in the middle of August, I had talked to Mr. Olsen in his office, confiding in him my disappointment over the closing of the door to travel through Russia, and asked if he thought it possible for me to escape with my three children over to England. Mr. Olsen was sympathetic and optimistic about the possibilities. "However," he said, "I'll only send you on a good boat where there is a cabin for you and the children. When I'm confident that I have such a boat, I'll let you know."

Meanwhile people escaped every week in all kinds of boats. With the Gestapo closing in on them, many Norwegians desperately fled, often in unsafe boats.

On a few occasions some of these, mostly young people, came and told me that they would be escaping the same night. I didn't understand why they took a chance in telling anyone. Perhaps they sensed they could depend on me and wanted to confide in someone. Whenever that happened, I spent most of the night deeply concerned about them and praying that they would have a safe journey. Months later in London, I learned that they had all arrived safely.

Ola Olsen and Dr. Sigurd Hus Help Plan Our Escape

Two months later Mr. Olsen contacted me. About 9 o'clock Monday morning, October 27, I heard a knock on my kitchen door. It was Peder Stavland who lived on the upper floor. He had just come from his office, and brought a message from Ola Olsen: "Come to my office at one." It could only mean one thing, the chance to escape which I had been waiting for since August. But now with my hopes near fulfillment, I felt frightened and weak. Sitting down a few moments to regain my strength, I considered the decision to be made. Then determinedly I put on my coat, hat and rubbers, grabbed the umbrella and hurried out into the cold rainy morning towards Mr. Olsen's office.

Being the business manager at Rubbestadnes Diesel Motor Factory, Mr. Olsen had a private office. I knocked on the door and heard a "Come in." I opened it and walked in, carefully closing the door behind me. The conversation about to take place was not for other ears. Ola Olsen greeted me solemnly. With a grave expression on his face he confided, "A boat came unexpectedly last night from Lerwick, Shetland, and is returning tonight. It brought a secret agent from England to Norway. If you want to go with your children as it returns to Lerwick, I believe there is a possibility it can be arranged." It was a big decision, but it was also the opportunity I had hoped and prayed for. Without hesitating, I answered, "Yes, I'll go."

He told me it was a good boat, a seventy-foot cutter, manned by the Royal Norwegian Navy in exile, and it was armed. He added, "Not one of our boats has been attacked by the Germans, but, of course, there is always the possibility of being spotted by a Nazi airplane."

As we were talking he received a phone call from Bergen. Concluding his conversation, he remarked, "There will be a lady, a nurse, on the trip, and also three young men." That was all he said. Later I learned that on the phone call Mr. Olsen had been informed that three big boxes and one small box were being shipped from Bergen.

Actually it meant three men and one woman were coming who needed help in escaping the country. Because they never knew who might be listening on the phone, they had to use a code system. Before leaving the office, he told me to come back in the afternoon to make sure everything was going according to plans.

On my way home I dropped in to see my mother-in-law and told her my plans. I then hurried home to pack. Since I could take along only two small suitcases, I had to sort out the most necessary clothing. Edward was only fourteen months old, so most of it was for him. When the older boys saw me packing, I told them we were going to visit my mother in Arendal.

Later I returned to Ola Olsen's office. On the way I met Dr.

Sigurd Hus. He stopped his car for a moment and in a low voice said: "I understand you're going on a trip tonight; I'll pick you up at 9 o'clock." Being a doctor, he was one of the few people who was allowed to use his car. Besides using it to visit his patients, at night he would also help people who had to escape the clutches of the Nazi tyranny. I proceeded to Mr. Olsen's office. He told me everything was in order for our escape that night, and he wished me God's blessing for a safe journey. Once again I returned home.

The boys and I were ready and waiting for Dr. Hus at 9 o'clock, but he didn't arrive until 11 p.m. He explained there had been a delay at Lervik, Stord. One of the men from Bergen had not shown up, and they finally had to leave without him. So besides the boys and myself there would only be the nurse and the two young men as passengers.

Because of strictly enforced blackouts, only two tiny lights were permitted on the car. We drove in silence. It was a long ride. Before we reached the shore, the doctor stopped the car and told us to proceed by foot. Seemingly out of nowhere, somebody appeared and guided us in the dark, down to the dock where a small motorboat was waiting for us. Immediately it set out from shore, headed for the fishing cutter which was anchored farther out, hidden between little islands. Not a word was spoken. Utmost care had to be taken as we never knew when German or Norwegian spies were around. We were safely brought on board the cutter *Siglaos*.

Dr. Hus helped us aboard and as he shook hands with me, he said: "Drop me a line when you arrive in the United States, so I'll know you've arrived safely." I promised. Little did I know that before we would reach our destination, Pearl Harbor would be attacked and Germany would declare war on the U.S.A. It wasn't until 1945 that I could write to anyone in Norway!

As soon as we were onboard *Siglaos*, it weighed anchor and we were on our way! It was midnight. I felt relieved and believed the worst was past. I had no suspicion of what was to come.

We were led to the rear of the boat to the cabin we were going to occupy. On the deck there was a door which opened up to a stairway and at the bottom of the stairs was another door and it led to the cabin. When we were taken down to the cabin, I noticed a crew member place some machine guns over in a corner, and heap our bags on top. Thus far they hadn't needed the guns in their many crossings between the Shetland Islands and Bremnes, Norway.

Safely on the boat, I told the boys that we were on our way to Dad. They were jubilant! Edward hadn't seen his father as yet, but Roy and Leif had missed him very much. It was calm when we set out, but as soon as we had passed the last skerries, the wind began to blow, and the sea grew more and more violent. The small boat rolled continually from one side to the other.

I had put the children to bed as soon as we got settled in the little cabin. Miss Hofstad, the nurse, occupied one end and Leif the other, in one berth. Roy was lying in one end and Edward and I opposite him in the second berth. The two young men were given quarters with the crew in the front of the boat. Roy, Leif and I were seasick, and I spent most of the night caring for them.

Siglaos is Attacked

Towards morning I dozed off but awoke when I heard an explosion right next to me. I thought a torpedo had hit the boat, and my first thought was to run up on deck to find out what had happened. When I opened the bottom door, I saw big holes in the upper door, and heard an airplane and the tic-tacs of machine-guns. I hurried back to the berth and Edward.

During a lull in the shooting one of the crew members managed to sneak down to our cabin. Frightened, I asked him, "What is happening?"

"We are attacked by a Nazi plane; they flew away, but they will be back," he answered. "Do you know where the guns are?" he asked. "I saw somebody put them over in that corner and pile our suitcases on top," I answered, and pointed to the corner. He grabbed the guns and started to load them. He sat on a drawer which had slipped out from Leif's berth, due to the rolling of the boat. He sat facing the door. Meanwhile the plane returned and again opened fire. The cabin door flew open and during the split second, the Nazi threw something down which exploded and lit up the whole cabin. The shock forced the gunner to his knees, but he was unharmed.

Once more the plane flew away and the man was able to get up on deck with the loaded guns. For the third time the plane descended and attacked with machine-gun fire, but this time our men were ready and returned fire. The plane then disappeared and did not return.

However, the plane had inflicted heavy damage on the boat and the twenty-three year old helmsman, Nils Nesse, was fatally wounded. The batteries for electrical equipment were shot to pieces, so for the rest of the trip, we had no light in our cabin or elsewhere onboard. The boat was leaking and soon the floor in our cabin was covered with water. The Nazis likely reported Siglaos as sunk.

Never in all my life have I been so frightened as when I heard the firing of machine-guns and the explosion of the hand grenades in our cabin stove. I thought it was the end for us all and I was gravely concerned for the children. I turned to God in prayer, and as I prayed, it was as if a still small voice spoke to me and assured me that not a hair on our heads would be touched! A wonderful peace settled over my whole being. I realized as never before that God was our Father, who loved us and would help us through all difficulties. It was as if the little cabin was filled with the presence of the Lord.

After the plane disappeared, we continued our journey. The nurse went on deck to see if there was anything she could do for Nils Nesse, but he was already dead. Nobody talked about the horrible moments. The children were awake during the attack, but they too appeared calm and were quiet.

The crew of five, now reduced to four, had to man the pump constantly to keep the badly leaking boat afloat. Only once after the attack did the captain come down to our cabin to see if we were all right; he was too busy with the boat.

I had taken some sandwiches along with a quart of milk which Grandma Terdal had given us. Only once was I able to get hold of the milk to give Edward some, otherwise none of us had any food or drink during the trip. Because we had no light, the nurse would light one of her matches each time I had to change pants on Edward. When the matches were gone, we were in constant darkness.

It was Wednesday forenoon, October 29, when we finally arrived at Lerwick. The trip had lasted for a day and a half. We had managed without food or water, tossed about in a terrible storm, and endured the horrible experiences of an enemy attack.

No sooner had the boat docked than people from ashore came down to our cabin to help us. British soldiers took the children and our bags ashore. Leif had only one shoe on. I found the other shoe floating on the water-covered floor. Before leaving the cabin, I looked around. I saw bullet holes all around the upper parts of the walls. Bullets had penetrated the walls on one side, passed through the cabin, and gone out the other side.

Miraculously none of us had been hit in the cabin. God in his infinite mercy had kept us safe. Then I too left the cabin and was assisted to the deck where we all were greeted by the Norwegian Consul and the British army personnel. Seeing me they smiled, and I was told that my face was covered with soot. It was from the explosion in the pot stove close to my face.

The British army captain, whose mother was Norwegian, had been stationed at Lerwick because he spoke Norwegian and could be of great help to the refugees. He was at the dock to greet us and apologized because they came to pick us up in an army jeep. During the night, in one of the worst storms in years, the garage roof had collapsed over the car. He took us to a building where a Catholic priest offered good hot tea from a big gallon container. The children were given milk and English Biscuits. It tasted good to all of us, but especially to Edward, who was so thirsty that when the milk was consumed, he drank tea like a good Englishman.

Not until we had eaten did the officials ask for permission to inspect our belongings. A couple of soldiers went through our belongings very thoroughly, searching even my Bible and handbag. They kept our passports, issued by the Nazis, which we had been compelled to carry with us at all times in Norway. Also they took the written statement I had received from the German officer in Bergen, which stated we would have permission to leave Norway when an opportunity arrived. Of course, escaping to England wasn't included in the permission. I would really have liked to have kept it as a souvenir.

Although they searched our belongings thoroughly, they were friendly and courteous; we were with friends, not enemies. I was told that this examination of our belongings was a routine performance, for among the refugees were also Quislings, who came to spy.

The army captain was concerned about our well being. At first he wanted the boys and myself admitted to the hospital to make sure we were all right. As no room was available, he called different places until he placed us at a "Mission to Deep Sea Fishermen."

Before we were brought to the Mission, we visited the refugee camp. It consisted of barracks used during peace time by girls who came to Lerwick to can sardines. At the camp were many Norwegian men and women, who had previously escaped from Norway. They were interned until passage to London was available. Having heard about the attack on our boat, they were glad for our safe arrival.

Soon an army jeep arrived, picking up the children, myself and the baggage and drove us to the Mission where we were to stay. They assigned us to the hospital room which had twelve beds. We occupied one corner of the large room.

Because of the war, deep-sea fishing had been halted and thus service men in the armed forces, stationed at Lerwick, were assigned the large reading room on the main floor. They came to read, write or just relax with a cup of tea. They enjoyed playing with the boys even though they couldn't understand each other as the boys spoke only Norwegian. These service men frequently brought candy and other goodies to the children. Some told me they had been down to the dock and seen *Siglaos*. They said there was a big hole on one side of the boat right above the water-line, and commented that it was a miracle we had reached shore. The Germans had consistently fired at one place to make a big hole so the boat would sink. *Siglaos* did sink at the dock a few days after our arrival.

Those in charge of the Mission were wonderful Christian people. They did all in their power to make our stay with them as pleasant as possible.

Because Leif had a cold, an army doctor examined him and prescribed medication. He was an elderly, dignified and very kind doctor. He continued his visits. One day I said: "Leif is fine now."

"I know," he said, "but I just wanted to see the children. How I wish all the children of Norway were here."

We ate our meals in the army dining hall after the soldiers had eaten. To us who had been used to meager rations of poor quality, the food tasted delicious. The friendly atmosphere was overwhelming. We were picked up in an army jeep at the Mission before every meal and brought to the dining hall. After the meals we were allowed to visit together with the other refugees for awhile before returning to the mission. The boys enjoyed this as they spoke only Norwegian and at the Mission everybody spoke English only.

One day while we were eating, I noticed an army officer watching us. I was puzzled, but when we finished the meal and walked outside, he came over and said: "It must be very lonely for you and the children to be at the Mission all day; would you like to visit my wife and little daughter?" I accepted his kind invitation, and he arranged for a jeep to take us to his home. They were living in an impressive old castle while he was stationed at Lerwick. His wife and daughter were most charming and the invitation was open to visit them anytime, but someone had to drive us anyplace we went, I didn't want to impose on them any more than was necessary.

One day the crew from *Siglaos* visited us at the refugee camp. They were in dress uniform of the Royal Norwegian Navy, for they had come from the funeral for Nils Nesse. A sad day for us all; but we were glad to see them. We were told that we were the only refugees who had been allowed to meet the crew afterwards.

While in Norway I had been sure that once safe in England, it would be easy to fly from there to the United States via Lisbon, Portugal. But, at Lerwick, I was informed that travel between Lisbon and London was restricted to important military personnel only. Learning that no civilians were permitted was a great disappointment. After our experience of the airplane attack crossing the North Sea, the thought of crossing the Atlantic Ocean by boat scared me. I began to realize that getting over to the Shetland Islands was only the beginning of a long journey. I was greatly disturbed and wondered if perhaps I had made a mistake by leaving Norway. The step had been taken, however, and there was no return.

After one week we left Lerwick on a big passenger ship for Aberdeen, Scotland. I was told that the waters were mine-infested. Once the crew had a machine-gun drill. After the machine-gun attack on our little boat in the North Sea, the noise from the practice was so unbearable I felt like screaming. Roy, too, remembered the shooting on the Siglaos and it was agonizing to see the fearful expression on his face. But the trip was completed with no incidents.

In the evening we arrived at Aberdeen, where we were escorted to a hotel and treated very kindly. When the Norwegian Consul at Aberdeen, Mr. Sandvik, visited us, I told him of my shattered hope to fly to Lisbon and from there to New York. Consul Sandvik suggested that when we got to London, I should get in touch with Mrs. Biddle, the wife of the American Ambassador. Maybe she would be able to help me.

The next day we left by train for London, escorted by detectives, a man and a woman. They shared the compartment on the train with the children and myself. They were friendly, helpful and kind during the journey.

A Month Waiting in London

Arriving in London we were once more interned. The men and the women refugees were now taken to different quarters. Along with twelve women, the children and I were confined in a large old building. With food differently prepared than we were used to, Edward became quite sick. Vomiting and diarrhea prevented him from retaining any food. The sympathetic hostess told me I could have whatever I wanted for him, but I couldn't hurt her feelings by telling her that the food was too highly seasoned for a small child. I asked for a doctor, but none came. Finally, to get medical attention for Edward, I pleaded to let the children and myself be sent to the Norwegian government in exile. My request was granted and we were taken in a taxi to County Hotel. Once more we were together with Norwegians.

The first person we met in the lobby was my husband's cousin, Carl Hoegberg. I didn't know he had escaped from Norway. He said afterwards: "When I saw you walk in with your three children, I could feel my face turn white." Carl had done what so many of the Norwegians did, leave their families, flee to England, with one thought in mind; to help liberate their homeland from its oppressors. I learned that he was one of the many who manned little boats making frequent trips to Norway with ammunition and agents. He was one of the few who was still alive when the war ended. It was a most dangerous mission.

After we ate dinner, we were escorted to Jenkin's Hotel nearby where we were going to live. The County and Jenkin's Hotels were leased by the Norwegian Government in exile for the duration of the war. County Hotel was very large. Seamen and service men stayed there on their time off from duty, likewise male refugees until they were assigned their duties. At Jenkin's Hotel lived families and single girls. Everybody ate in the large dining room at the County Hotel. No meals were served at Jenkins. Everyday we walked four or five blocks to County Hotel for our meals. Our rooms and board were paid for by the Norwegian Government.

The next day after arrival at Jenkins, a Norwegian doctor examined Edward. He prescribed thin tea, with milk added when Edward was able to retain it. Soon he was well again.

Later I went to Western Union, where for the first time I was able to send a message to Alf that we were in London. While we were interned by British authorities we weren't allowed to contact anyone. They had to be sure we weren't spies. I certainly appreciated their cautiousness for one never knew whom to trust.

When I went to register with the Norwegian government in exile, I met a Norwegian journalist. Seeing my three small children, he asked: "Have you just come from Norway?" When I answered yes, "Yes," he exclaimed: "We must have your story in the newspapers!" I replied: "We left Norway in utmost secrecy and I'm not going to have it published that we escaped. I want to protect those who made the escape possible." The journalist assured me that there was no danger of exposing anyone in Norway, for as he explained: "We don't mention where you came from in Norway, and we give you a fictitious name." When I was told this was the usual procedure, I consented, but refused to have our picture in the papers.

As I was interviewed by him and he learned about our dramatic crossing from Norway
to the Shetland Islands, he again begged to have our picture in the papers. I finally consented to have Edward's picture taken as there was no picture of him in Norway. The journalist called me Elsa Johansen and the following Sunday the story of our dramatic escape and Edward's picture appeared on the front page of all the large London newspapers.

An English journalist came to the hotel and wanted a picture of all of us for his paper. He pleaded with me for a long time, but when he realized the futility he commented:

"If all the Norwegians had been as firm as you, maybe Norway wouldn't have fallen under enemy occupation."

One of the personnel at the Norwegian Information Office told me that they had been flooded with phone calls and mail inquiring about our well being and offering help if needed. He then said: "For your safety's sake, we haven't let any of them contact you personally." The minister's wife at the Norwegian Seamen's Church in London gave me a baby stroller. This was a great help as we lived in one hotel, but ate at the County Hotel. This was the only gift I accepted.

My main concern was to get passage to the United States. I tried Nortraship, which was in charge of Norwegian shipping, but with no result. Remembering that Consul Sandvik at Aberdeen Scotland had suggested I contact Mrs. Biddle, I wrote her a letter, which she referred to the U.S. Embassy. I had an interview but they weren't able to help. Two weeks after we had joined the Norwegians in London, I received a telegram from America. It said: "See Fenrik Olsen, Airforce, Kingston House, concerning passage to United States." Signed Arne Feroy. Mr Feroy and his wife and two children had been our tenants at Rubbestadneset. He had escaped several months before us and his family had moved away from Rubbestadneset.

I phoned Fenrik Olsen, told him my plight, and read the telegram I had received; he suggested I come to his office at Kingston House. Mr. Olsen was a very busy man for it was he who interviewed the many young men who had fled Norway and desired to go to Toronto, Canada, and join the Norwegian Royal Air Force in exile. They all had one common goal – to free Norway from its Oppressors.

After listening to my story, Mr. Olsen seemed optimistic about helping us to get passage to Canada, for he arranged passage for the young airmen. However, it wasn't as easy as it seemed, for the captains on the Norwegian freighters, recognizing the danger involved, refused to take women and children.

Mr. Olsen told me to continue coming to his office, in case

there should be an opening. It was a long trip on crowded buses. At first I took all three boys with me. Later some of the refugee women offered to care for Edward in exchange for my help with their shopping as they couldn't speak English. Roy and Leif continued to accompany me every time.

I also went to the U.S. Embassy to register the children, who were American citizens, and to inquire about a visa for me to enter the United States. The assistant ambassador told me to return when I had booked passage, and then I would get the visa. I left confident that this would be no obstacle.

Meanwhile life went on in London. We got used to the routine of living in one hotel and walking several blocks for our meals at the County Hotel. The huge dining room was always crowded. The food tasted very good to us refugees. Edward especially enjoyed breakfast for he loved oatmeal. The then fifteen-month old boy had observed his brothers saying grace. He probably thought that saying grace brought the food to the table, so as soon as we were seated at the table, he folded his hands, bowed his head and said: "Blah, blah, blah." If the food hadn't arrived yet, he continued his "prayers" until the food was on the table, to the delight of the other guests.

As time passed other refugees arrived. Many whom we knew from Bremnes had to flee because the Gestapo, having learned about their underground activities, were doing their utmost to catch them and throw them into concentration camps. Among them were some who had helped me and my children the night we left Norway, but because of darkness and silence I hadn't known who were the helpers.

One morning as we were walking to the County Hotel for breakfast, I stopped at a newsstand to buy the morning paper. The man at the stand pointed to the headlines. In bold type across the front page stood, "JAPANESE ATTACK PEARL HARBOR!' It was December 7, 1941.

I had hoped so very much that we would be united with Alf for Christmas, but as time passed, I realized it would be impossible.

Mr. Olsen had, however, given me a slight hope that we might be able to leave for Canada around New Years on a Norwegian freighter. I was admonished to tell no one, including the children for security reasons.

U.S. Embassy in London Hesitates Giving us a Visa

A couple of days before Christmas as I again went to Mr. Olsen's office, he gave me the good news that the captain on a freighter had consented to take us on his ship to Canada. It was a tremendous relief. I had just about a week in which to get ready. When I went to the U.S. Embassy to get a visa for myself, I happily told the assistant ambassador I finally had attained passage and asked for a visa. He replied: "I can't give you a visa now; I must have permission from Washington."

Frustrated, I exclaimed: "I have struggled for almost two months to get passage, you mustn't stop me from leaving now." In desperation I added: "My husband has been in constant touch with Washington since we arrived in London." Without saying a word he went into another room, came back with a telegram in his hand and remarked: "This came yesterday." He then read it to me, "When Mrs. Terdal comes to your office, give her all the assistance she needs for a passage to this country."

He felt it was quite a coincidence, but I felt the good Lord was watching over us and guiding us every step of the way.

Since we had to spend Christmas in London, I planned to make it as festive as possible for the children's sake. The other refugees with children suggested that we join together for a little party on Christmas Eve. Someone bought a Christmas tree, and we received some decorations at County Hotel.

Since I spoke English, the Norwegian office for the refugees asked me to go to the Red Cross center and pick up Christmas gifts for the children.

Christmas Eve arrived and about twenty people assembled in the hotel living room. Some of the single men and women had asked permission to join us. We sang the Norwegian Christmas carols we all knew so well, and I'm sure all of us were thinking about our loved ones in the enemy-occupied Norway. The children eagerly opened their gifts, some toys to play with as well as useful articles.

After singing Christmas carols and the children had opened their gifts, I said: "I have never celebrated a Christmas Eve without the story of Jesus' birth having been read." From my Bible I read the wonderful story of a Savior who was born as related in the Gospel of Luke, second chapter. When I was finished reading, I led in the Lord's Prayer.

Since two days later, on December 26, was Leif's fourth birthday, I treated them all to buns and coffee. After having been used to the food in occupied Norway, our appetites were easily satisfied.

In the few days between Christmas and New Year, I was busy making final arrangements for our departure. I wired Alf to send money immediately for our travel expenses. I made several trips to the American Embassy to gain permission for the boys and myself to travel to the war zone. Then at night I lay awake worrying if we would reach the American continent.

For strict security reasons nobody knew we were leaving. A couple of days beforehand, I was told that we should leave London in the morning of New Year's Day. We were told to travel by train to Swansea on the British channel where we would board s/s *Brant County* the following day.

On the evening of New Year's Eve, the children and I went to the County Hotel for our last dinner in London. During the dinner in the crowded dining room a representative from Nortrashship gave a speech and thanked the many seamen for their courage and sacrificial contributions to the cause of their homeland.

Just then a seaman I had seen around during our two months stay in London created a scene. Having broken an ankle in the line of duty, he had been walking with the aid of crutches and had remained sober. Now, to celebrate the removal of his cast, and to celebrate New Year's Eve he had been drinking. After the

Nortraship representative had finished his speech, this seaman yelled loudly, almost hysterically, about the many Norwegian seamen being sunk by the Nazi submarines and fighting for their lives in the icy and stormy Atlantic Ocean.

Worn by worry over our journey across the Atlantic Ocean, and from the many tasks completed for our departure, I almost lost control of myself. I too felt like screaming. It took all the restraint I could muster to sit silent and pretend he made no impression on me.

After dinner we went to our hotel room, where I told the boys that we were leaving the next morning to travel to dad. Roy and Leif were very happy, Edward had not seen his father yet and was too little to understand.

Elsa Haldorsen, whose husband is related to Alf, had escaped from Rubbestadneset two months before us, but had been unable to proceed to Toronto, where her husband was an instructor in Little Norway, a Norwegian Airforce Base, teaching young Norwegian

Refugees to fly or maintain airplanes. When Mr. Olsen got passage for the children and myself, he also arranged for Elsa to travel on the same boat. While Elsa was in London, she had been a guest in the home of the treasurer of the bank of Norway.

We had only two suitcases, which were full when we left Norway. During our two months stay in London, we had acquired a few articles of clothing and some toys. Since I couldn't fit it all into the suitcases, I had to pack some, mostly toys, in paper bags. Because of the war there was an acute paper shortage in England and the available paper was of very poor quality. We had to save our paper bags and bring them with us to the stores when we went shopping.

New Year's morning Elsa Haldorsen and the bank treasurer came in a taxi, picked up the children and myself and our belongings and took us to the railroad station. As we left the taxi, the bottom dropped out of the paper bag and the various articles and toys were strewn on the sidewalk. Looking back upon the incident, it seems funny, but at the time I was dreadfully embarrassed as the bank treasurer helped me gather the stuff and somehow we crammed it into the torn paperbag.

We boarded the train without further incident and arrived at Swansea in the evening. Mr. Olsen had given us the name of a hotel where he would make a reservation for us. To our dismay we discovered that he had forgotten, and there was no vacancy in that hotel. They suggested another which we set out to find, not an easy task in a strange city at night with a very strict blackout. Finally a policeman helped us and gave us the right direction. How frustrated we were to hear again, "No vacancy!" I presume we didn't look too attractive, at least not the children and I, for we had been using the same clothes, more or less, for two months. While silently praying to God for help, I pleaded with the receptionist and finally she gave us one large room where we all slept. That was sufficient for one night, and once more we were taken care of.

Next morning we took a taxi to the dock. In the daylight we could see the city. It was a frightful sight! Most of the buildings were in ruins. The taxi driver told us that the Germans had repeatedly bombed, aiming to sink the many ships at the docks. They had missed the target, however, hitting the city and civilians instead.

We Board the s/s Brant County

With mixed emotions I boarded the ship together with my children and Elsa Haldorsen. I was happy because finally we were on our way to the United States and to husband and father. But facing the stark reality of the dangers involved in crossing the Atlantic, I was frightened. If it hadn't been for faith in God and the privilege of prayer, I couldn't have faced the situation.

On board we met the officers and crew and were escorted to our cabins at the midships house. On deck level were the officers' quarters, the pantry and the captain's dining room. Above that the captain had his quarters, which consisted of a living room, bedroom and bath. One more flight up were three passenger cabins where we were going to stay. The next flights up led to the navigation bridge.

s/s *Brant County* was a freighter. Westward to Canada she carried some coal, mainly for ballast, but returning to England she was loaded with ammunition, a dangerous cargo indeed.

The captain of the ship, Captain Brevik from Bergen, greeted us and wished us welcome onboard. He was a husky man who carried tremendous responsibility. We soon learned that he was a kind and friendly man as well. After orienting us as to rules and regulations onboard ship, he invited us to join him for our meals. The dining room was a combination dining room and living room and we spent most of our time in that room during the crossing. Whenever the mates, radio operator, chief engineer and the steward had time, they came there to talk with us and to play with the children. Because they hadn't seen Norwegian children since they left Norway before the war, they enjoyed playing with them, especially Edward, who was seventeen months old and quite lively.

They also had many questions to ask about conditions in Norway since they no longer received letters from their loved ones.

Soon after we had boarded the ship we weighed anchor, but we went only a short run in the Bristol channel where we anchored. Other ships were also lying at anchor, and we were informed that we were waiting for more ships as we were going to travel in convoy. As we walked on deck we saw masts sticking up in the water. They belonged to ships lying at the bottom, sunk by Nazi bombers. Would there be any flying over and attacking us while we were there? Luckily none appeared. More ships gathered and after a day or two we proceeded north and again anchored, this time in the vicinity of Belfast, Ireland. This was the final stop where all the ships met and were given orders and their places designated in the convoy.

On January 5, 1945, sailing orders were given and the ships started to move. Before long each ship was in its designated place in the convoy. It was a clear sunny day and the forty ships escorted by the impressive white British warships were a magnificent sight. The sea was calm. With the many ships together plus the large warships, we began to feel secure even though a bloody war was going on.

Attached to the masts of the ships were blimps. The wires on those blimps were so strong and sharp that they could cut off the wings of any airplane that might fly into them. They provided some protection against air attacks.

The weather remained sunny and calm for three or four days. Spending some time each day on deck, we became acquainted with the crew. In the afternoon of the fourth day as we were walking on the deck, we noticed the British warships circling among the tankers and freighters and signaling to them with flashlights.

The captain called to us from the bridge: "You can watch the men remove the blimps. We have received orders to take them down because a storm is in the offing."

"Oh," I said, "I thought this was a warning of submarines, and I was frightened."

"We must take the bad with the good, Mrs. Terdal," was his reply. I soon learned the truth of it.

Soon it became stormy and by nightfall the storm had intensified. The raging wind tossed the ship to and fro like a nutshell in the mountainous waves. While the children slept peacefully, I lay awake hour after hour, praying to God for help. A verse from the Bible brought me some comfort: "I will never leave thee, nor forsake thee."

Suddenly, about 5 a.m., the ship's whistle blew; once, twice, three times! I jumped out of bed and awakened the children. Elsa rushed from her cabin. "What is it?" She asked.

"When we were in London," I replied, "I heard seamen mention if they had spotted a submarine they blew the whistle to alert the crew."

"What shall we do?"

"Get dressed, put on lifebelts and hurry downstairs," was my reply.

We got dressed hurriedly. Noticing the fearful expression on Roy's face, I tried to reassure him: "Don't be afraid; Mother has been praying all night and God gave me the comforting word, 'I'll never leave thee nor forsake thee.'"

Outwardly I appeared calm as I comforted my children, but silently I spoke to God: "Is this the reason you gave me that scripture verse, for this is the end, but you promised to be with us?"

Elsa, Roy and Leif got their lifebelts on, but I carried Edward's and mine as we hurried downstairs. As we came to the captain's quarters on the deck below, we saw light in his living room. I knocked on the door, and at his, "Come in," I opened the door and we went in. Weak with fright and from carrying Edward and the lifebelts, I dropped into a chair nearest me. The captain was resting on a couch. He looked puzzled and a flicker of a smile appeared as he saw us all dressed and with lifebelts.

"What is the matter?" he questioned.

"We heard the ship's whistle and thought there was danger," I replied.

The captain eased our fears as he explained that he had been on the bridge all night because of the storm. The convoy had split up because the heavy storm and high sea prevented its staying together. But one oil tanker right in front of our ship was experiencing difficulty in moving because of the high sea. The whistle was a warning signal to it.

"But," said the captain, "It's only a few minutes since the whistle sounded." He seemingly was impressed because we had been ready in a very short time.

We returned to our cabins. Later we understood the captain had mentioned the incident to the officers. They made no remarks about it to us, but there was a certain expression of respect and admiration on their faces, for during it all we had appeared calm. The only one who mentioned the incident was the steward. He assured us that if ever a time should come, during the crossing, when danger was imminent, his first duty was to help us and get us safely downstairs.

Whenever a convoy wasn't able to stay together, all ships had to proceed on separate courses due to the lurking dangers of submarine attack. During that long night, the British warships and all the tankers and freighters disappeared except the one tanker which was directly in front of us. Soon that one too disappeared, and from then on we saw no other ship. However, the radio was constantly manned to receive warnings of submarines and orders to change course to avoid submarines.

The storm continued to rage. When we ate I tied Edward to his chair lest he should fall. Otherwise we sat on the floor, for the constant tossing to and fro of the ship made any movement dangerous.

The crew had stretched a heavy rope on deck from the front to the rear of the boat which they could hold on to when they had to cross the deck. One nineteen-year-old sailor was hit by a huge wave which washed over the deck. The force of the wave threw him around. Although he was rescued and carried inside, he died shortly after of internal injuries. The next day this young man was buried at sea. He was the second to die during our journey, the first being Nils Nessa, killed by a Nazi bullet in the North Sea.

The storm continued its violent course, moving in cycles. For a day the storm would diminish slightly, only to increase its velocity worse than ever. Once the chief mate commented: "I can give you some consolation, it can't get worse."

Our Convoy is Attacked by German Submarines

Over the radio the operators continually picked up S.O.S. from ships which had been torpedoed and from one ship which had split in two due to the storm and the heavy sea.

The officers told us about the S.O.S.'s they received and each time my heart cringed in anguish. Because Roy also heard them talking, one day I asked them: "Please, don't tell us about the S.O.S.'s you receive. It's hard on Roy for he understands." But we continued to hear about them anyhow.

As the waves constantly washed over the ship, extensive damage was done to it. One of the lifeboats was washed overboard. It became evident to us that even the officers doubted that we would reach shore, but they did their best to put up a front for our benefit.

To top it all, one day the news came over the radio that Germany had declared war on the United States. As the captain discussed that sad event, he added: "We usually considered ourselves safe as we came closer to the United States, but now this is really becoming a danger zone, for the German submarines are infesting the coastal waters of the States."

One day Leif complained about pain; both his lower cheeks were swollen and he was running a temperature. It looked like mumps. The captain looked at him and was sure it was mumps, but I wasn't convinced. Before boarding the ship we had signed papers that we realized there would be no doctor onboard. The chief mate had studied First Aid. He looked at Leif and then said: "Let's hope it's mumps, but somehow I don't believe it is." (When we arrived in the United States, we found out that he suffered from a bad case of tonsillitis and swollen glands.) The poor four-year-old boy remained sick for the rest of the trip, but he was very patient giving way only to an occasional little moan. Previously chubby and with a good appetite, he now ate very little and grew thin.

Feeling that it was more than I could endure, at times I thought my mind would crack. With Leif running a temperature, how could he survive if we ever had to go into a lifeboat? As a matter of fact how could we get into a lifeboat in that storm-raging ocean?

However, despite the difficulty in standing and the enforced sitting on the floor day after day, the boys behaved wonderfully. They never complained and everyone on the ship remarked about it and marveled at them. It was only when Leif got sick and started to cry and said: "I want to go home; I want to go to where I came from." The captain, sympathizing with the little sick boy answered: "I have given orders to turn around and go home." Poor

Leif, he didn't know that even if he wanted to, we could never return to Norway as long as the Germans were there.

At the beginning of our journey, I undressed the boys at night, but let them sleep in their underwear. As the storms and dangers increased, I removed only their shoes; otherwise they were fully dressed. The mate questioned me one day as to what I did with the children when I put them to bed at night. "I remove only their shoes," I said. "leave them on too," was his advice. "If we should have to go in the lifeboats, it's very important to keep the feet warm." From then on I didn't even remove their shoes, but the thin worn shoes we all had wouldn't have kept our feet warm very long.

As for myself I had remained fully dressed the whole trip except for my shoes. I slept very little. Exhausted I would fall asleep in the evening for a few minutes, only to awaken and remain awake for the rest of the night. I wasn't afraid to die; as a matter of fact, there were times when I felt it would have been a relief to sink down in the ocean and worry no more. But my three children were constantly on my mind. I felt if I should lose one of them I couldn't bear to live. I thought of Alf waiting for us in New York.

During the long nights I was in constant prayer. The Bible verses I had memorized down through the years were a constant source of encouragement, but my faith was weak. I was still so very much afraid and worried.

As we came nearer to America the weather improved markedly. One day I could even take Roy and Edward out on the deck for a short time for a breath of fresh air. Leif had to remain inside because of his illness. My growing hope of reaching shore soon received a jolt as the captain called to us from the bridge: "This is a beautiful clear day. Be on the lookout for submarines."

Wanting to encourage me, the chief mate invited me to the chart room to see our location on the chart. Our destination was St. John, New Brunswick, Canada, but we were then located east of New York City. He pointed to a straight line to St. John and said: "We are only five hundred miles from port."

I complained: "The distance between England and Canada is three thousand miles. We have been traveling for two weeks, and you say we'll soon reach St. John. Yet there are still five hundred miles left."

To this he answered: "We have zig-zagged the Atlantic, constantly changing course because of submarines. We have covered twice as many as three thousand miles.

"But if we now have to change course?" I asked.

Very soberly he commented: "We can't change course any more. From now on we're headed directly for port."

As the weather continued to improve, the ship proceeded with full speed. Then a few days later jubilantly we were informed that they saw the lights of Nova Scotia! We were entering the Bay of Fundy which meant no more dangers. The submarines couldn't reach us anymore!

My feeling of joy and gratitude is indescribable. That evening I could at least undress the children and give them sponge baths. Not once during the voyage had I dared to undress them or bathe them. Happily I said to Roy: "Two more days and we'll be with Dad."

"Two more days and we'll be sunk," was his grave answer. That was the first time he let me know that he had realized the danger we had been exposed to.

It was a bitterly cold night, but when the children were sleeping, I went on the deck to watch the lights from the distant shores. My heart was filled to overflowing with thanks and praise to God for having kept us safe from all harm.

After having spent so many sleepless nights, I still couldn't sleep, but I didn't mind lying awake freed from the fear of disaster. It took months before I was able to sleep restfully, for I continued to wake up worrying about the many who were braving the elements and were facing constant danger of enemy attack.

Our Ship Arrives in St. John, New Brunswick

The following day we docked at St. John, New Brunswick. The

third mate then told us: "Usually I don't pray, but on this trip I have prayed that God would keep us safe for the children's sake."

The steward added: "I said, if there is a God, let us reach shore for the children's sake."

They all had shown us pictures of their loved ones in Norway. Although they knew nothing about their safety, they had been concerned for us.

It was bitterly cold in Canada. The water pipes on the ship froze, causing additional problems for the men onboard.

Upon arrival there was a telegram waiting for me from Alf requesting me to phone him immediately. I wasn't allowed to go ashore and use the phone until the ship's agent came and escorted me to a phone in the office. He warned me not to mention anything about our journey, including the stormy weather and what time we had arrived in St. John. He stood beside me during the conversation with Alf to be sure no information leaked out to any possible listeners on the line. It was great to hear Alf's voice again after more than a year and a half. There were so many times during the journey when I didn't believe I would ever hear it again.

After the phone call, the agent expressed his surprise that the captain had taken women and children along because of the dangers involved.

Likewise the captain declared that because of the great danger he would never again take women and children along. January had been a particularly disastrous month at sea. Many of the ships which had started out with us in the convoy never reached their destination. The captain also said it was one of the worst crossings he had ever made.

The captain had earlier told me that his cousin, Miss Clara Brevik, was a House Mother at the Norwegian Seamen's Church in Brooklyn, New York, and he requested me to visit her when I came to New York, and deliver a letter which he had written to her.

The next day we said "Goodbye" to the brave men on s/s *Brant County* and to Elsa Haldorsen, who was going to meet her husband in Montreal. We boarded a train for Boston, Massachusetts, where we changed train for New York. We arrived at Grand Central Station on January 27, 1942, three months to the day since we had left Norway.

Our Family is Reunited

Alf met us at Grand Central Station. What at times seemed impossible had happened, we were together again as a family; it was hard to restrain the tears. The boys were overjoyed to at last be with their father again.

With Alf was also Irene Haakonsen who, with her husband, Johannes, had invited us to stay with them until we found a place to live.

Of first importance was to get Leif to a doctor as he was still sick. Upon Captain Brevik's advice we had not consulted with a doctor in Canada for that would have delayed us and we were anxious to get to New York and to Alf. Leif was suffering from tonsillitis and swollen glands. In March his tonsils were removed and he gradually recuperated.

News of our arrival immediately leaked out. Somehow the Norwegian Information Bureau in New York had been informed about our arrival, (How, I'll never know), and the following day I received a telegram from them asking for permission to interview us.

At the same time I received a telephone call from one of the Norwegian churches in Brooklyn, asking if I would come and speak to their church. I declined the speaking engagement for so soon after our harrowing trip, I just couldn't consider speaking in public about our experience.

Representatives for the Norwegian Information Bureau, however, came to Haakonsen's home for an interview. With them was a photographer who insisted that since it was now three months after our escape, no one would be endangered by publicity or news photo of us. They also used the name Elsa Johansen which had been given me in London. They invited us to a press conference at Waldorf Astoria. One of their representatives called for a car and took us to the Waldorf where we met representatives from the various New York newspapers who interviewed us. Also present was Mrs. Gladys Petch, who at that time had a weekly program about Norway on the municipal radio station. She urged me to appear on her radio program. At first I declined, but upon stronger urging from the Norwegian Information representatives, I consented. Mrs. Petch arranged for me to be on other networks. Over the nest weeks I appeared on four different radio programs. The Norwegian Information Bureau wanted to rent a hall in New York City and have me speak, describing the conditions in Norway under the Nazi regime, and our escape, but I declined.

Leaders in the Norwegian churches began to ask me to speak in their churches. After giving it thoughtful consideration, I decided that when God had been so merciful towards us, the least I could do was to tell others about his mercy.

My first speaking engagement was at my church, the Bethelship Norwegian Methodist Church in Brooklyn, New York. The church was filled to capacity with people standing in the hallway. It was a moving experience to me, for when I had finished telling about our escape and the dangers it had involved, the choir sang, "God is still on the throne, and He remembers his own." During the many long nights when I was filled with anxiety for my children's safety, I had sensed God's presence in a real way.

I continued speaking in churches in Brooklyn, Queens, Staten Island and New Jersey, telling them about our experiences and God's marvelous grace and protection during those difficult times.

Knowing that we had left all our belongings in Norway, our friends decided to have a shower for us. One evening in February about seventy people gathered in Haakonsen's home while I was visiting next door. Some of the guests were complete strangers to me, who, having heard of our adventures, wanted to help. When I was called back to the house and saw all the people, I was overwhelmed by my emotions. During the long, long nights while crossing the Atlantic, I had resigned myself to the thought that I would never again see our family and friends. I rushed past them and into the kitchen where I started to cry. My sister, Hedvig, put her arm around me and comforted me: "Don't cry, these are not Nazi's, they are your friends." It was a thrill to see them all and to open the many beautiful and practical gifts.

We rented a house, bought furniture, and moved in. But soon afterwards our friends, the Henriksens, informed us of a house for sale next to theirs in Staten Island on Sawyer Avenue. We liked it, bought it, and it has been our home since.

When I visited Miss Clara Brevik in the Norwegian Seamen's Church and gave her the letter from her cousin, Captain Brevik, she urged me to write to the captain and the crew of the ship as they couldn't get any mail from their families in Norway. So I wrote a letter to Captain Brevik and thanked him and everybody on the boat for their kindness to us during the three weeks we spent on the ship. His reply is among my cherished possessions. He wrote that he had posted my letter on the ship's bulletin board for everyone to read, for the crew often talked about us. He added: "You were very brave and courageous." He never realized how scared I had been.

In 1943, on a trip to England, loaded with ammunition, s/s *Brant County* was hit by a torpedo and sunk after a terrific explosion. A seaman who had been on another ship in the convoy told me about it. Only a few of the men were rescued; the rest went down with the ship. Among them was the captain, who left his wife and two daughters in Bergen, and the chief mate, who left a bride. He had married just before leaving Norway in 1939 and the war prevented his return.

* * * * *

In 1954 I revisited Norway for the first time. I visited the parents of Nils Nesse, the young man who had been fatally injured during the attack on our little boat in the North Sea. They had asked me to visit them, but it was very difficult to tell them about the happenings that early morning when their young son was killed.

I also took a trip to Oklandsvaagen, where we had boarded the fishing cutter Siglaos that night on October 27, 1941. I walked up on a hill and stood there gazing over the ocean and the little islands which hid the boat from the enemy. My heart was full to overflowing with thanks and praise to God who had protected us through a long and dangerous journey.

Chapter 8

THE SHETLAND BUS

The term "Shetland Bus" refers to the traffic across the North Sea during the Nazi occupation of Norway from 1940 to 1945. Norwegian fishermen and other crew transported agents and military equipment from the Shetland Islands to Norway, and brought refugees and persons who sought training to assist in fighting Germans from Norway to Shetland.1 The Shetland Islands lie in the Atlantic ocean about 200 miles west of Norway. Many residents are of Scandinavian ancestry, and Norse customs remain prevalent. Norwegians referred to the Shetland Islands as "England" rather than a part of Great Britain. The Shetland Islands are the most northerly county of Scotland. Our own crossing on the Siglaos in October 1941 represents one such crossing of the "Shetland Bus traffic." It was one of our two dangerous sea crossings. Our other was crossing the Atlantic from London to St. John, New Brunswick, a passage referred to as the "North Atlantic Convoy Traffic."

My memory of our crossing is limited to what a four year old could understand. I remember that late one night we did not go to bed and mom was nervous and kept looking out the window expecting a car to appear. Dr. Hus finally arrived, we got into his car and he drove in the dark without headlights. We got into a fishing boat and headed out to sea. The ocean was rough so we sat on the floor because the boat rocked too much for us to sit down on the benches. As the first light came the next morning, we heard the loud engine of an airplane and then rapid fire gunshots. Bullets burst through our cabin. One man was dead. I understood that more gunshots could kill more of us. My little brother Edward, fourteen months old, got hungry and wanted to be fed. Mom was burdened and distracted by the extreme danger, and was not focused on food for any of us. With no food coming Edward muttered a prayer that we always said before a meal, carefully taught by our mother. A portion of the prayer in Norwegian goes as follows: *I Jesu Navn gar vi til bords a spisr og drikke pa ditt Ord. De Gud til aere, oss til gavn.* The English translation is, "In Jesus' name to the table we go, to eat and drink according to his Word. To God the honor, us the gain." After his prayer, little Edward, 14 months old, looked up expectantly for food. (I don't mean to imply that Edward spoke in even two word sentences, he did not, but he muttered sounds as though he did when together we prayed out loud before a meal.) I remember thinking that he did not understand we were in trouble. I thought I knew the danger, but I did not. At age four I did not understand that our boat could be sunk with all lives lost. However, we made it all the way to Scotland.

Our crossing in October 1941 occurred eighteen months after the military defeat of Norwegian and Allied forces in Norway. Norwegians were confronted with the presence of a huge German occupation force of more than 350,000 troops and the knowledge that German forces had quickly overrun a number of European countries. Furthermore, the Norwegians had reason to fear (as did the British) that German forces might also invade and conquer England. These crossings of the North Sea during war time in fishing boats were not authorized by the Norwegian government (which was in exile). The Norwegian government in exile certainly favored and supported the Shetland Bus operations, but the system was developed independently, quite spontaneously and without much organization. In time, a number of groups were organized to help those who wished to escape.

Our own escape was made possible by coordination from a group in Bergen known as the Kristian Stein organization. Members of this group maintained secret communications with others including one in Bremness on the island of Bomlo. There Ola Olsen, the office manager at the Marine engine plant in

Ruabbestadneset, Dr. Hus and a Lutheran minister coordinated crossings. No written records of contacts were kept, nor names of fellow resistors. The fear was that if Germans would uncover a list of names of Norwegians involved in the resistance movement, then all would be at risk for arrest and/or execution. The secrecy was such that when my mother and her three children boarded the *Siglaos* she was not to know the names of the other people on board – and certainly not their reason for escape. Even the captain did not know the names of his passengers. He knew the persons on board his vessel had been authorized for the trip by Mr. Ola Olsen and Dr. Hus. The reason for the secrecy was that in the event of a capture, a passenger (or crew member) on one of these vessels would not be able to provide critical information to a German Nazi even under threat of death. The level of threat during the occupation was severe.

Our escape is recorded in a book written by David Howarth, *The Shetland Bus: A WW II Epic of Escape, Survival, and Adventure.* The following excerpt portrays the level of secrecy that was maintained as Dr. Hus brought a group to board the *Siglaos*, including my mother with her three sons. In Howarth's account, Gunderson, the captain of *Siglaos* is waiting for Dr Sigurd Hus, a central figure in the Norwegian resistance on the island of Bomlo.

...the doctor returned in the evening with two men, two women and three children. One of the women, the mother of two of the children, was the Norwegian wife of an American citizen who had escaped a year earlier. She had been lying low in Lervik waiting for a chance to follow him. The other woman was a Norwegian nurse who had been in the Channel Islands when they were invaded. The Germans had kept her for four months in a prison in France, and had then sent her back to her own country; and ever since her arrival there she had been trying to get back to Britain. On the strength of these two stories Gunderson agreed to take them all, though he never found out who the two men were, or the third of the children.2

Later, Howarth describes weather conditions and the air attack on *Siglaos,*

They left Oklandsvaag just before midnight on 27 October. On their way over the weather had been bad, but now it was worse. A whole gale was blowing from the north-west, on their starboard bow, and by dawn they were only fifty miles from the coast. As the first grey light came into the sky they sighted a twin-engined aircraft to the southward. Gundersen was in the charthouse, Nesse at the wheel, Bard Grotle, the engineer, in the engine-room. The rest of the crew and all the passengers were in the cabin.

At the time our boats were armed with anti-tank rifles, Bren guns and tommy guns, the Brens being mounted on detachable mountings on the deck. But the weather was so bad, with seas sweeping the deck, that all the arms had been taken inside and lashed down. Before anything could be done to mount them the aircraft turned, approached Siglaos at mast height from astern, and opened fire with cannon. ...

Nils Nesse had stuck to the wheel throughout the attack, but they saw him fall. He was hit in the head and the leg. With the help of the nurse they bandaged his wounds and carried him to a bunk, but there was no hope that he would recover. He died an hour later without regaining consciousness.

*Siglaos had continued under way during the attack, and when the nurse had attended to Nesse, Gundersen put the boat on its course again and inspected the damage. ... The upper works and lifeboat were riddled with shell holes, the sails in rags, and the mizzen mast cut nearly through, but the hull itself was undamaged.*3

Our trip on the *Siglaos* was very dangerous, and as described above it caused a great deal of stress to our mother, who had three young children aboard this effort to escape. She describes her reaction in Chapter seven. However, with this account as a background, let us consider an overview of the saga of the Shetland Bus and the crossings over the North Sea. Who were the Norwegians who left and what were their motives? The authors Ragnar Ulstein, 4 David Howarth 5 and Trygve Sorvaag 6 agree that many were young men and women who left for Shetland with the expectation of joining Allied forces to return to Norway to fight and drive out the Germans. This widely anticipated invasion, of course, did not happen. Other Norwegians who escaped did so out of fear they had been singled out by the Gestapo for capture and detention. Still others left because they could not tolerate the Nazi occupation and took the risks involved. In the case of my mother she had no plans to join a military force, nor did she feel she had been singled out by the Germans. She, of course, wanted to be reunited with her husband in New York, but she especially wanted to raise her three children away from Nazi influence.

In 1940 about 56 boats escaped and with them 548 people. In 1941, the year of our escape, 191 boats crossed the North Sea, carrying 2388 people.7 Not all the boats survived, and some of the losses were the result of weather. About two weeks after the *Siglaos* left the small harbor of Oklandsvagen on the Island of Bomlo, the fishing vessel *Blia* with 43 people on board left Oklandsvagen. In addition the vessel *Arthur* had left a nearby port. On November 10, 1941, a storm broke out and steadily increased in intensity. David Howarth describes the storm as reaching wind strength of over 100 miles per hour and lasting a full five days. The *Arthur* had left on November 8 and was expected to arrive in Shetland on the tenth. The storm caused considerable damage to the base at Shetland. Many seaplanes were sunk at their moorings and ships were driven aground. The *Arthur* had been within hours of landfall before the storm hit. Incredibly it made no forward progress for five days. It was battered with waves breaking over the deck, over the cabin and over the stern during the seven-day storm. The crew constantly had to bail and do what they could to keep the engine going. One crewman was lost overboard. On November 15, the vessel finally came in to port. The mast had broken off and was lying astern. Gun mountings had been swept overboard. Down below was a chaos of broken pottery and scattered food. But, except for the one crewman, all on board made it to shore. The captain of the *Arthur* was Leif Larsen. This skilled, resourceful and courageous man made a total of 56 North Sea crossings during the war. Those aboard the *Blia* were less fortunate as all 43 were lost at sea during the terrific storm, making its loss of life the most suffered of any single voyage from Norway to Shetland during the war.8

The following year (1942) only 17 boats left Norway to cross over to Britain, because the seaports along the west coast of Norway were shuttered down as they experienced a more severe kind of storm. 9 The storm was reminiscent of one that hit Lidice, a village in Czechoslovakia, on June 10, 1942.

The Telavag Tragedy

My mother with her three sons arrived in New York City on January 27, 1942, after our ninety days in transit from Norway. In the United States my parents could receive no information from Norway, as communication was cut off by the Nazi occupation. It was not until the end of the war that my parents began to hear about the events and tragedies that had occurred in Norway after our departure. Some of the tragedies were beyond comprehension. The destruction of the community of Televag is but one example. The German forces were intent on stopping the North Sea traffic; they placed posters at fishing harbors throughout western Norway declaring that contact with the enemy (England) was punishable by death. This, of course, included efforts to escape to England. The Germans increased their surveillance along the west coast and interrogated many Norwegians.

In April 1942 German infiltrators had information that two agents had arrived at Telavag from England (Shetland). Televag is a small community on an island just south and west of Bergen. The Germans knew the identity and location of the family protecting the agents. At night German troopers barged into the house where the agents and family were asleep. The agents were quickly aroused and fired against the Germans, killing two high-ranking Gestapo officers. One of the agents was killed during the brief action; the other was executed. The reprisal by the Germans was severe. The Germans arrested all the males in the community above the age of 16. Those captured were required to watch as

German demolition personnel used explosives to destroy several of the houses in Telavag. The captives were then sent to a German concentration camp where they faced brutal interrogation and torture and remained there until the end of the war. Thirty one perished, others were physically and mentally brutalized. The women and children were then required to witness the destruction of the remainder of the community. Every house was blown to pieces. All the vessels in the harbor were destroyed. The women and children were then interned for two years at Hardanger. Telavag had been obliterated.10 The small community was restored after the war and is now pristine, and it is the center for an important museum which provides historical information about the Shetland Bus, the destruction of Telavag, and the brave men and women who provided effective resistance during the occupation.

Information obtained by German infiltrators during this time was not restricted to Telavag. Germans uncovered information about the most effective resistance organizations involved in the Shetland Bus operations. For example, the network between Bergen and the Island of Bomlo was uncovered. This resulted in the arrest of Mr. Ola Olsen, Dr. Hus and many others.11 The key coordinator in Bergen, Mr. Stein, was executed. 12 Mr. Olsen was placed in a concentration camp in Norway and tortured. One method the Germans used in an attempt to break down the will of Mr. Ola Olsen was the capture of his son. Mr. Olsen was then told by his guard, "Mr. Olsen we have captured your son! ... You answer our questions about resistance leaders in Norway, or we will kill your son!" Mr. Ola Olsen replied, "Kill me, but not my son. However, I will tell you nothing!"13

Dr. Hus also faced brutal torture during his imprisonment in a concentration camp in Germany, and he never regained his health. The Shetland Bus network had ceased to exist by1942, with the leaders dead or in prison.14

The British recognized the importance of the North Sea traffic and the military benefits that had been achieved. For example, David Howarth writes that over 60 radio transmitters were sent back to Norway along with trained men/women to track and transmit information about German troop movements and naval activities. Hundreds of tons of military equipment were shipped to Norway via the Shetland Bus. In addition, Norwegian spies informed the British about the heavy water plant at Rjukan. Furthermore, the Norwegian seamen had expert knowledge about the Norwegian coastline, its hazards and its deep water channels. The British were well aware that they completely lacked this vital information during the failed allied military offensive of April and May 1940. By the summer of 1942, further use of Norwegian fishing vessels to handle the North Sea traffic was no longer possible. Numbers of experienced Norwegian seamen who had transported people and equipment back and forth were land-locked in the port of Scallaway, Shetland Islands. All struggled with the question of how to proceed. 15

Suddenly the answer came. Howarth notes that Admiral Nimitz, Commander-in-Chief of the American Naval Forces in Europe, learned of the situation and sent an order for three U.S. Navy sub chasers to be sent to headquarters at Scalloway, Shetland Islands. 16 Soon three ships arrived. These ships were 110 feet long and cruised at 17 knots, rather than the 5 knots of the fishing boats. Each was powered by two 1200 hp diesel engines, in contrast with the one large displacement single cylinder engine producing about 40 horse power on most of the fishing boats. Each ship was well equipped with central heating, fully equipped galley, hot and cold water showers and many other features. These ships named *Hessa*, *Hitra*, and *Vigra* were manned and operated by the same Norwegian seamen who had operated the fishing boats. They completed missions successfully from 1943 until the end of the war.

It is beyond the scope of this book to review details of the military objectives that were achieved by Norwegians who took part in the Shetland Bus operations. To cite a single example, one Norwegian, who had been trained to observe German naval operations, transmitted by radio exact information to the British about the location of the German Warship *Tirpitz*. This led to the British successfully destroying this, the last German battleship, in November 1944. 17

A critically important sabotage action was accomplished in March 1943 when Joachim Ronneberg was dropped by parachute over the Hardanger plateau between Oslo and Bergen. He and eight other men from the Linge group blew up the Norsk Hydro's electrolysis installation for heavy water at Rjukan. All nine men were able to ski themselves to safety and to return to Shetland for more assignments. This successful sabotage ended the Nazi plan to build a nuclear weapon. 18

Chapter 9

NORTH ATLANTIC CONVOY TRAFFIC

After completing the first of our two-part travel by sea in our escape from Nazi-occupied Norway, my mother was fearful of crossing the Atlantic by ship, as she remembered the airplane attack while crossing the North Sea. Her fear came back as we were driven past major sections of London that remained devastated by German bombing during the autumn and winter of 1940. Then on January 5, 1942, we boarded our ship, the s/s Brant County, and our ship moved in position to join the other ships in our convoy making a total of 40 ships. Once on board my mother saw masts sticking out of the water, which belonged to ships previously sunk by Nazi bombers. She was somewhat relieved to see that our convoy was escorted by large warships; however, she had good reason to be fearful.

The scene that my mother witnessed reflected a reality of the importance of shipping to England. England must import large quantities of oil, food and other materials to survive both in peace time and in war. The initial war strategy of the Germans was to block all shipments to England by sinking British merchant ships, as well as any foreign merchant ship headed for England.

The U.S government, recognizing the vulnerability to the British merchant fleet on March 11, 1941, passed the Lend Lease Law, which provided for the supply of war materials and other goods, the repair of British ships, and the initiation of large scale ship building programs in the US to cover the mounting losses of merchant ships during wartime. The US also increased production of escort vessels and aircraft to monitor convoys. [1]

The purpose of this section is to provide a brief overview of the Battle of the Atlantic to put in context both the importance of merchant shipping during wartime, and the extraordinary efforts to protect the fleet on the one hand and the sustained effort to destroy the ships on the other hand. As I have reviewed the historical records, I have been impressed by the rapidity of change of strategies and the pattern of losses. In his analysis of the Battle of the Atlantic, historian Jurgen Rohwer identifies one phase as beginning July 1, 1940, and continuing to December 11, 1941. With the conquest of Norway and France, Germany gained control of the entire coastline of Norway and the west coast of France as naval bases. These bases were critical for the German military. They offered both more security and much closer access to military targets against England and the North Atlantic convoys. Given this opportunity the Germans began to move U-boats, surface warships and supply ships away from Germany to bases in Norway and France. 2 German control of the port of Narvik also ensured Germany access to critical supplies of Swedish ore.

At the beginning of this period the Germans had a limited number of U-boats, although many were under construction. Furthermore, during this same period the Germans did not have long range aircraft to cover far reaches of the Atlantic to search for convoys. On the other hand, the British were so concerned about an expected imminent attack on England that they held back their powerful navy to protect the homeland and let the convoys travel without protection.

In September 1940 a number of the available German U-boats were sent far out into the Atlantic to gather weather reports for the planned Operation Sealion, the code name for the invasion of England. On September 20 one of these submarines spotted convoy HX.72 consisting of 41ships. With the help of four other U-boats on the same weather mission, they sank twelve ships. A month later ten U-boats deep in the Atlantic encountered convoy SC.7 and sank 21 ships; the same submarines later sank twelve ships from convoy HX.79.

Following these disasters to unescorted convoys, the British military concluded that the expected German invasion of England had been cancelled. Abruptly, the British changed plans and began to use warships to escort the convoys. This had an immediate effect of successfully protecting the convoys. The Germans with a limited number of U-boats, changed plans and withdrew the submarines and sent powerful German war ships to attack the convoys that were now under British escort. 3

The Germans sent four powerful battleships into the fray: the *Scharnhorst* and *Gneisenau* displaced 32,100 tons, had a top speed of 31 knots and had nine inch guns. The *Admiral Scheer* and the *Admiral Hipper* were comparable in displacement, speed and weaponry. On November 6 the *Admiral Scheer* attacked convoy HX.84 and engaged in battle the British auxiliary cruiser *Jervis Bay*. In a protracted battle the 37 ships had time to disperse. However, the *Jervis* Bay was sunk as were five ships of the convoy.

The *Admiral Hipper* attacked convoy SLS.64, sank seven ships, and then returned to a German base in Norway. The *Scharnhorst* and *Gneisenau* searched the Atlantic over a two-month period and sank or captured 22 ships from dispersed convoys before heading back to a base on March 23, 1941.4 About this time the Germans made available the Fw-200 Kondor four-engine, long-range aircraft to act as spotters in the Atlantic to communicate positions of convoys and escort vessels to U-boats and German surface warships. 5

Operation Rheinubung

Operation Rheinubung was a bold German plan to devastate the North Atlantic convoy traffic. In this operation the *Scharnhorst* and *Gneisenau* were to enter the North Atlantic and join with the *Bismarck* and *Prinz Eugen* who were to steam from Norway to join forces. They were to be supported in their planned attack on convoys by a fleet of support vessels including seven tankers, two scout ships and several weather observation ships. However, prior to the rendezvous British air attacks severely damaged the *Scharnhorst* and *Gneisenau* so both had to be withdrawn from the planned action.

On May 20, 1941, the *Bismarck* and *Prinz Eugen* were discovered and photographed in the Grimstad Fjord south of Bergen by a British Spitfire spotter aircraft. On May 22 another British spotter plane found the Fjord empty. 6

In perhaps the most significant naval battle in the Atlantic, the Commander-in-Chief of the Home Fleet Admiral John Tovey directed a plan of attack that led to the sinking of the *Bismarck*. The battle spanned 1750 miles of ocean and resulted in the sinking of the British battleship *Hood* with the loss of Admiral Holland and 1417 crew. The new British battleship *Prince of Wales* was severely damaged but was able to continue contact with the fleet before returning to port for major repairs. Admiral John Tovey was able to organize a massive search and hunt for the *Bismarck*. In addition to the *Hood* and *Prince of Wales*, the cruisers *Norfolk*, *Suffolk*, *Sheffield* and *Dorsetshire*, the battlecruisers *Renoun*, *King George V*, and the *Rodney*, the destroyer *Maori* and two aircraft carriers, the *Arc Royal* and the *Victorious* were involved in the sinking of the *Bismarck* with the final death throes on May 27, 1941. Admiral Lutjens, the German commander, the entire fleet staff and 2,106 crew went down with the *Bismarck*. 7 The British rescued 115 survivors. The historian Rohwer writes,

At 1035 hours, after she had been hit by two torpedoes from the cruisers Norfolk and Dorsetshire, the crew fired the explosive charges in the turbine compartment and the Bismarck went down to the bottom on an even keel. ... The ship lies at a depth of more than 11,000ft, and the photographs show the extent to which all the superstructures and guns of the ship had been destroyed before she sank, and therefore how great must have been the loss of human life before she went down. 8

During this battle the British captured the weather observation ship *Munchen*, and U-boat *U 110*. These two captured vessels had on board coding documents. 9 The British decoding center at Bletchley Park was able to decode the classified information, which led to the capture of six of eight German support vessels that had been sent into the Atlantic to support the now aborted operation Rheinubung. The decoding center at Bletchley Park continued to decode information sent to German U-boats, which made it possible for the British to direct convoys away from the known locations of German U-boats. Thus, in the second half of 1941 the British convoys were able to cross the Atlantic with reduced losses. 10 December 11, 1941, is considered the end of the effort by Germany to rely on surface ships to destroy the convoys crossing the Atlantic. The next phase was based on U-boats in the mid-Atlantic, and a major new focus on convoys in the Arctic and Northern Norway.

In December 1941 the British launched a major raid against German positions in the Lofoten Islands, which lie off the coast of Norway and north of the Arctic Circle. In addition, the Germans were aware that the British were shipping large amounts of military equipment (lend/lease from the US) from Iceland to the Russian ports of Arkhangelsk and Murmansk. The German Naval Command shifted strategy and sent all available surface ships to northern Norway including the newly commissioned battleship *Tirpitz* and the repaired *Scharnhorst* as well as a number of U-boats. The Luftwaffe force was strengthened to include Ju-88 bombers and He-111 torpedo aircraft. 11

Long stretches of the Atlantic during the period from December 1941 and on were patrolled by an increased number of German U-boats but no German surface ships. It was this level of German coverage that our convoy went through in January 1942. During a six-month period from January 1, 1942, through June 30, 1942, the German U-boats sank 1000 ships in the Atlantic. The United States was now in the war and 497 of the lost merchant ships were sunk off the East coast of the US by German U-boats in Operation Paukenschlag, with a loss of only seven U-boats. 12 Although the British had the capacity to decode information from the Germans, our convoy was hit as was described in my mother's account. This can not be a surprise. With the added focus by the British on threats to the convoys going to Russia and the US entry into the war, the entire war scenario changed, and the convoys crossing the Atlantic were increasingly vulnerable. Furthermore, the Germans had launched a large number of newly constructed U-boats to enter the fray.

Convoy PQ. 17

In early July 1942 convoy PQ. 17 set sail from Iceland to Murmansk. It was escorted by US warships for part of the trip and British warships as the convoy approached the Arctic seas of northern Norway. On July 4th the British received a report that the *Tirpitz* had been directed by the German Naval Command to intercept the convoy. With that threat the British First Sealord ordered the convoy to be broken up and dispersed, with no further protection by British warships. German U-boats and aircraft sank twenty-four ships of the dispersed convoy of thirty-six ships. Hundreds of seamen were lost as well as the cargo of 430 tanks, 210 aircraft, 3,350 military vehicles and 99,316 tons of material. This was part of US lend/lease to Russia. The *Tirpitz* had never left port. 13

The s/s Brant County is Sunk

In February 1943 the Germans changed the code they used to transmit information from ships at sea to German bases in Europe. The British could no longer warn convoys about the location of German U-boats in the Atlantic. On March 2, 1943, the *s/s Brant County* departed Halifax on a voyage to Liverpool in Convoy HX 228 with 60 ships. The convoy was escorted by 2 British and 2 Polish destroyers, 2 British and 3 French corvettes, as well as an aircraft carrier with 2 American destroyers. On the evening of March 10, U-boats attacked the convoy and an intense battle ensued and continued throughout the night. The British destroyer *Harvestor* was sunk as well as 6 ships of the convoy, including *s/s Brant County*.

At 2:30 AM on March 11th the *s/s Brant County* was hit by a torpedo and the ship began to list almost immediately and took on water. The ship was aflame. In twenty minutes the fire reached the compartment holding tons of explosives. The ship then blew apart, and Captain Brevik and 35 of his crew were killed. There were some survivors. Through my son, Paul Terdal, who was able to search internet for names of survivors of Norwegian Merchant ships lost in WW II, I have been able to contact Ken Ballard and his son Barry Ballard some 62 years after the war. I also sent along to Ken Ballard a copy of my mother's account of our escape from Norway.

Mr. Ken Ballard sent me a copy of his contract to work on the s/s *Brant County* including the signature of Captain Brevik. It was a remarkable experience for me to see that document. Mr. Ballard is a citizen of England and was hired to help man the ship. The crew was largely Norwegian. Mr. Ballard told me that it was his habit during any warning of an attack on the convoys to stand topside on the deck. This was because the explosion of a torpedo could warp the ship and make it impossible to open steel doors down below. That habit, he says, saved his life. When the torpedo hit he was at the stern of the boat hanging on to the rail. He jumped into the water. The night was very stormy, and the waves were very high. When the ship exploded the ship was down in a trough and he was down in a trough on the other side of a large wave that provided a buffer from the terrific explosion. Because he worked on a Norwegian ship during the war, Mr. Ken Ballard received a thank you note from the Norwegian government and he receives a pension.

During WW II Norway turned over one thousand ships to the British for use in the war effort. No Norwegian ship at sea returned to Norway after the German invasion. Of those one thousand ships used by the British, over five hundred were sunk. In addition to Captain Brevik and his crew of 35 who were killed on the s/s *Brant County*, 4,500 Norwegian seamen lost their lives in active service at sea. They transported 145 million tons of cargo of inestimable value to the Allied victory.

Passport photo taken summer of 1941 when mother hoped she could get a commercial trip out of Nazi-occupied Norway. From left to right, Leif, Edward and Roy.

Photo taken in Oklandsvaagen on the Island of Bomlo, Norway where we departed for the Shetland Islands on the night of October 27, 1941. Photo taken about fifty years after our escape. From left, cousin Leif Helland, son Paul Terdal, Leif Terdal and grandson Finn Terdal.

Photo taken at St Olaf College. Mr. Ola Olsen, a major figure in the Norwegian resistance meets with our family whom he helped. Parents Harriet and Alf Terdal, sons Leif, Edward and Roy (seated). Photo taken about twenty years after our escape.

Grave site of Dr. Sigurd Hus with my parents Harriet and
Alf Terdal and Ola Olsen (center). Both Dr. Hus and Olsen
experienced brutal torture during incarceration by German forces.
Dr. Hus died of his injuries.

Brothers Edward, Leif (standing) and Roy meet and reflect on war, resistance to war, and family. Photo taken about fifty years after our escape.

Leif, wife Marge Terdal and Leif Helland enjoy the patio cafeteria of the Televaag Resistance museum near Bergen. Televaag, now rebuilt, was entirely obliterated by German forces and all males over age 16 were sent to Nazi concentration camps where many died and all were tortured. Photo taken sixty-five years after our escape.

Part III

LIFE EXPERIENCES AND REFLECTIONS
AFTER THE WAR

Chapter 10

LIFE EXPERIENCES AFTER THE WAR FOR LEIF, ROY AND EDWARD

When we arrived in NYC in late January, 1942, my parents were soon in contact with the Norwegian Bethelship Methodist Church in Brooklyn, New York. They arranged for us to home stay with a Norwegian family who had settled in Staten Island. We stayed with the Haakonsen family for about two weeks before people from the same church helped my parents find a home for my parents to buy. My father had a good income as a chief engineer on an oil tanker, operating out of one of the harbors in Staten Island. On Sundays we drove to the Staten Island ferry and crossed over to Brooklyn to attend church services that were still spoken in Norwegian. We adjusted to life in the U.S. rather quickly even though not one of us three brothers knew a word of English upon our arrival.

Roy started third grade at P.S. (Public School) 30, about a one-half mile walk from our house. A few days after he started school, my mother got a call from the Principal, who had a complaint about Roy. Roy had copied the answers on an exam from the girl who sat next to him. He even copied her name! My mother explained that Roy, his two brothers and she had just arrived from Norway and the children knew no English. The principal firmly advised: "Do not speak Norwegian in the home, otherwise Roy and your other children will not learn English." From that point on my mother and father spoke English (with a strong Norwegian accent) and only spoke Norwegian to us when an English word would not do.

I began first grade at P.S. 30 in the fall of 1943. By that time I knew enough of the English language so that learning at school was not a problem. By the time I was in third grade the school had "Parents Night." This was a time when a parent could go to school and meet with the school teachers and hear first hand how their child was doing. This began a ritual with an undertone of dread. Mom would speak at length with all the teachers that Roy had; then she would meet with my teachers. Then she walked home while we were all in bed. She first went into Roy's room and spoke with him about what she had learned of his school performance and behavior that needed improvement. Her tone was firm, uncompromising and unyielding. Roy had to do better, and she wanted no excuses. I remember thinking as I lay in the next bedroom hearing every word. "Roy must have really done badly, I wonder how I did?"

But alas, mom came to my bedroom. Again she spoke in a firm voice. She knew details of times when I was inattentive, or had not carefully checked my work. When Edward started school, it was the same for him. What mom was trying to say was school was very important and we must take it seriously.

We all had chores to do and mine included cutting the lawn and trimming the hedge. I found these chores often got in the way of important stuff like fishing in one of the local ponds (Martlins Pond) at Clove Lakes Park, or playing baseball with neighborhood kids. So, after cutting the lawn or doing other chores, A would ask mom, "How did I do?" She would look over my work and say in Norwegian, "Da va gonska gut!" With that approval, I was free to go and play.

When I was in sixth grade, I found myself in Miss Carston's Music Appreciation Class. On the first day of class, Miss Carston said, "We are going to learn some songs that our class will sing at the next All Parents Night. The class was excited! But first we were to sing, "Do Re Mi." The first day we sang "Do Re Mi" a number of times, but never got to learn a song. On the second day we sang it again, but learned no song. On the third day we sang it again and again. Finally, Miss Carston, looking a bit concerned, said, "I want each of you to come up to the front of the class and sing, Do Re Mi, while I play the tune on the piano." Because we all sat in alphabetical order, she started with a girl named Betty Andersen, and then the next child. I was the twenty-fifth child to stand up in front of the class to sing, "Do Re Mi." After each child had gotten up to sing, Miss Carston would smile then quietly dismiss the child to return to his/her seat.

When it was my turn, I knew I had a problem. I did not know the words of the song. I thought there were real words to a real song. It did not occur to me that "Do Re Mi" was a bunch of sounds that were not intended to give a message or tell a story. So, I tried to make sense of the sounds. I sang, "Do not ram me so far below sea." When the other

children sang, each one finished the tune at the very moment that Miss Carston finished playing the piano. In my case, I finished my words before Miss Carston stopped playing the piano. Miss Carston looked worried; she paused and said, "Leif, I want you to try that again." Now I knew that I had finished my song too early, and I was not certain that I sang loud enough for her to hear me. So this time I was ready. With a firm, but absolute monotone voice, I sang, "Do not ram me so far below the sea." By stretching out those words and not rushing through them, I finished at exactly the same time that Miss Carston stopped playing the piano. Maybe this time, my effort was good enough!

Miss Carston looked at me and said, "Leif, (pause) that is the worst I ever heard!" My knees slowly buckled to the ground, and I asked, "The worst you ever heard?" She paused …. then said, "Well there was another boy about five years ago, who was about that bad." She added with a firm voice, "You are not to sing in this class, and you will not sing during all Parents Night." After singling me out as the non-singer, she began introducing songs for the remainder of the students to learn.

I was crushed. I walked home trying to act as if everything was all right. As I entered the house, mom saw right through my bluff. She said, "Leif, what is the matter?" As she spoke Roy came into the room; he had just returned from Curtis High School. I said,

"Mom, Miss Carston said I was the worst singer she ever heard."
Roy, overhearing the conversation said, "Leif, don't worry about it.
She told me the same thing five years ago!"

News that Germany Surrenders

One day in May 1945, as I was walking home with a bunch of
neighborhood children from P.S. 30, a woman suddenly ran
out of her house and shouted with excited joy: "The war is over!
Germany has surrendered!" I ran home and told mom. She had
also just heard it. We were joyful and excited. My father found a
way to take a day off work and went to New York City to join a
massive parade.

However, the good news was followed by tragic news. During
the war my parents could not receive any mail from Norway. The
Nazi occupation force in Norway blocked mail delivery to any
country at war with Germany. I remember well the first letters
from Norway, after Germany was utterly defeated and surrendered. Mom got the mail in the afternoon and read through them.
She said nothing to us until dinner time. At dinner she said, "I
have a letter from Norway, I will read it to you a couple hours
after dinner." Outwardly she was calm. She did not want us to try
to eat with an upset stomach.

After dinner she called us to the living room. She opened a
letter, then said to us, "You remember Alma Helland your father's
sister in Norway, her husband Kristen Helland, and their children."
Of course we remembered. They were family as well as neighbors.
We had spent much time with them. Mom said, "One of their
young children, Gjert at age 8 had fallen off the dock near the
house we lived in and drowned. There were German soldiers
nearby, but did nothing to help." After much discussion and tears,
mom continued, "The husband of Alma, Mr. Kristen Helland also
died. He became sick with cancer, and could not get medical care.
He died in pain at home and without treatment."

Some weeks later, mom again called us to the living room
with a letter, "You remember Dr. Sigurd Hus." She continued,

"Sometime after he helped us escape, he was captured by the Germans and sent to a concentration camp in Germany. He was tortured by the prison guards in an effort to force him to give the names of other Norwegians who were active in the resistance movement. Dr. Sigurd Hus is still alive and back in Norway, but he is not well."[1]

Later she received word from Mr. Ola Olsen, that he too had been captured and tortured in a Nazi-run prison camp in Norway. Both Mr. Olsen and Dr. Hus were strong but kind gentlemen, who loved their country and bravely resisted the Germans who occupied their country. They were the ones who did the most to arrange for us to escape Norway.

Another day, mom said, "You remember the ship *Brant County,* and the brave captain Mr. Brevik?" She continued, "I have received word that the ship was torpedoed and then exploded with great loss of life among the crew. Mr. Brevik was one of those who died in the explosion of the ship. I learned by age eight, that when a war is declared over, it is not

really over. Tragic news may follow for years on end. I had a sense that none of us would ever get "over" the war.

My father was distraught by the news of the death of a son of his sister, Alma, and then also the death of her husband. When it was possible for him to travel to Norway after the war he made that trip, both to provide comfort and to find out what their needs were. He also visited his mother, who was so pleased to see him. She had lost her husband in 1912, and it was very hard for her to lose a grandson and a son-in-law thirty years later. They had a chance to review the struggles brought on by the occupation. During the late 1940's her health was good, although she was over eighty years of age. However, Ms. Anna Gjertine (Tina) Haldorsdaughter Terdal died in 1953, at the age of 87. She was a very special grandmother. As the oldest son, our father was to inherit the house. He flew to Norway and met with his sister, Alma Helland and her family. Quietly, he looked over the title and signed the house over to his sister knowing that she needed the house more than he needed the money from the sale.

My father and mother took many other trips to Norway to visit relatives, former neighbors, and to be observant at grave sites and memorials. On one of the trips they joined with Mr. Ola Olsen and visited the grave site of Dr. Sigurd Hus. This was especially difficult for my mother, because she knew that the life of Dr. Hus was taken as a result of his helping others like he helped our family. My parents also met with the family of Nils Nessa and reviewed the German attack on the small boat and the burial of their son in the Shetland Islands.

"Where the Women are Strong and the Men good looking"

You may be familiar with those words from Garrison Keiler, who speaks of the mythical Norwegian farmer town Lake Wobegon, Minnesota. Those words were very true in my family. My mother was always strong. She never displayed weakness. She had an outstanding ability to say what was on her mind clearly and effectively. By age twelve, I could say in absolute honesty that whenever mom and dad had an argument, that mom won. No exceptions. My father was no slouch. He was recognized as a top tier chief engineer. He was well read, and had a good grasp of history. At home, he was well cared for and a reliable wage earner. His children loved to listen to his stories, and to enjoy outdoor activities with him such as hiking and target shooting with a bow and arrow. In the Bethelship Norwegian Methodist Church, Pastor Johnson knew enough not to preach to his congregation that, "Wives should submit to their husbands." However, the local church in Staten Island was different. I paid careful attention to Sunday school lessons, and usually won the annual prize awarded to the Sunday school student who had successfully memorized the most Bible verses.

One day, when I was about 12 years old, I approached mom after one of her encounters with dad. I said, "Mom the Bible says that a wife should submit to her husband." Mom looked at me and without any hesitation remarked: "That does not apply to Norwegians!" My father would have agreed with his wife. He understood that his wife knew the school teachers, the doctors and the dentist, and the neighborhood families much better than he could have since his work on ships kept him away from home about two months out of three. On family issues she was better informed. The same is true for many Norwegian families and has been true for generations. In Norway the right to vote was gained by women decades before women in the U.S. could vote. After giving birth, a Norwegian mother is given one year's maternity leave with full pay. Norwegian women have had influence and clout since the Viking age.

Our family moved from Staten Island to Muskegon, Michigan, in 1952. The move occurred when an oil company in Michigan purchased the oil tanker that my father had worked on since 1941. My father helped run the tanker to Muskegon, an important harbor on Lake Michigan. The company hired my father to re-main on the tanker as the chief engineer. The tanker was renamed *Detroit*. I entered high school at Muskegon Heights. Roy had finished High School in Staten Island, and enrolled at St. Olaf College in Northfield, Minnesota.

Ola Olsen Speaks at St. Olaf College about Norwegian Resistance

While at St. Olaf College Roy called home to say that Mr. Ola Olsen had been invited to the college to make a presentation about Nazi-occupied Norway and the resistance movement. Mr. Olsen was unusually well qualified to have been an invited speaker at St. Olaf. He had been awarded a Gold Medal by King Olaf of Norway for his outstanding contribution in the Norwegian resistance movement. Although he had been arrested by the Germans, and endured torture, he did not break. It was an amazing coincidence that Ola Olsen had been chosen to speak at St. Olaf, while Roy was a student there. Our whole family was invited to attend, and we had several days to meet with Mr. Olsen and review our own escape and our lives afterward. It was clear to me that this very dignified and gentle man still lived with the on-going, painful memories of the tragic Nazi-occupation. Mr. Olsen knew details of many Norwegians who endured imprisonment and torture, and many who were executed. Approximately 30,000 Norwegians were incarcerated during the occupation. While at St. Olaf, Mr. Olsen reviewed the sad events of the imprisonment and mal-treatment leading to the death of Dr. Sigurd Hus.

After high school, I enrolled at Taylor University, in Upland, Indiana. I met Marjorie Starkweather, and I fell in love with her. We got married one week after graduation in June 1959. We moved to East Lansing, Michigan and I began graduate work in clinical psychology, and received a doctorate in 1965. We moved to Oregon, where I joined the faculty at the Oregon Medical School in Portland, Oregon. Marge gave birth to a son, Erik, in 1966 and to another son, Paul, in 1968. My work was focused on psychological assessment and treatment of handicapped children and helping parents cope with their child's disability and learn behavioral management strategies.

As a family we enjoyed travel and camping in the Northwest. In 1974, when the children reached the ages of six and eight we took the opportunity to take them to Norway to see that beautiful country and meet relatives. My father joined us for a cross country trip. He was our guide. We first visited Leif and Bitteba and their four children. In Oslo, Bjarne Helland took us to the Resistance Museum, the Vigeland Park, the museum of the Viking ships, the famous ships, *Fram* and *Gjoa*, used by the Norwegian explorers Fridtjof Nansen and Roald Amundsen. From there we drove the highway across the mountains over to Bergen. On the way we stopped to visit Bitteba's father on his farm in Hallingdal. His wife had been a school teacher in a one room school in the mountainous area of Hallingdal. She was one of the many teachers arrested for refusing to sign an oath of support of the Nazi occupation.

During all these fine visits I tried to express my appreciation with the remnants of the Norwegian language that I remembered. So after remarkable and tasty meals, served with fine Norwegian china, I often said, "Da Va Gonska Gut!" One relative, after hearing me say that numerous times, said, "I don't think you mean that." I said I meant to say, "The best ever!" He replied, "Well, what you said was, that was not good, but it will do." I had to rethink the numerous times I heard that expression from my mother.

Leif Helland, an engineer, showed us a large hydropower plant in the mountains built during the years 1942 and 1943. I asked, "How could Norway build these huge power plants during the war?" The answer was simple and stark. The Germans built the huge project with Norwegian money, and much of it with prison labor from Russia. Leif Helland reminded me that the Germans fully expected a thousand-year reign. Much of the electricity had been used for the heavy water project by Nazi engineers as part of their atomic bomb research program.

We traveled on to Bergen and visited Raidaer Helland and his family, and Annemor Helland Moen and her family. In Bergen our family was treated to a dinner in a fine hotel by my father's cousin Dr. Inger Haldorsen. She was aged but in good health. Her story is one of outstanding achievement and perseverance. As a young adult, in 1910, she was admitted to the Medical School in Oslo. To travel to Oslo before the age of modern transportation, she and her father rowed a boat from Rubbestadneset to Bergen. From Bergen she walked the two hundred miles to Oslo, over the mountains, in a twelve-day hike. There she completed her medical school training. During the war she refused to sign an oath that she supported the Nazi occupation of Norway. She was outspoken in her criticism of the occupation. She was arrested and placed in a Nazi prison camp in Bergen. After the war she was able to continue her medical practice.

We then traveled to Rubbestadnesset, where we had lived during the occupation and dad took us to the spot where we boarded the *Siglaos*. We also traveled north to Floro and to Terdal, a farm that has been in the family for four hundred years. On later trips I had a chance to visit my Cousin Helga and her husband Nils Finstad who live in Bodo; they also have a family farm in the Lofoten Islands. While there I enjoyed the opportunity to fish for cod and take trips on fishing boats like those used during the war to help Norwegians escape to the Shetland Islands. While visiting Helga and Nils Finstad, Nils told me that he lived as a child near a large prison camp, where Germans interned Russian soldiers captured during the early phase of the German invasion of Russia. He said that he and a number of other Norwegian children tossed food over the fence for the Russian prisoners. The children knew the prisoners were not fed properly.

My wife and I have also traveled extensively in Germany. During three different academic years, Marjorie Terdal, who has a Ph.D, taught at the University of Freiburg in southern Germany, near the Black Forest. We took many opportunities to travel within Germany as well as take excursions to Switzerland and France. On one occasion we took a train to Munich, to visit the infamous Dachau Concentration camp that is nearby. On the train I sat next to an elderly German man. In a conversation, I happened to ask him where he grew up as a child. He said, Dresden. I was startled, and I asked him in an uncharacteristic loud voice, "Were you there in February 1945, during the saturation bombing?" He commented that he had been visiting his grandmother in a nearby town, so he was away from the firestorm that killed more than 100,000 civilians. Dresden was not a military target; but in WW II both sides targeted civilian populations. The destruction of Dresden was like what had happened in Tokyo, in 1944 when over 100,000 civilians were killed in one night from saturation bombing that also produced a catastrophic fire storm. He looked at me and said, "I didn't know that you Americans knew about the bombing of Dresden." I then told him my story, and he listened courteously. He told me how proud he was as a youth to be part of the Hitler Youth program, and how much he regretted it later. He muttered several times, "I was so naïve, and so gullible!" Then he slowly said a word in German that I had not heard before. He said, "**Vergangenheitsbewaltigung.**" The word describes an act of coming to grips with the painful past, including the Holocaust.

Marge and I visited Dachau at a time when several hundred German High School students also were there to learn about the Holocaust. We understand that all German students are expected to visit at least one of the concentration camps. We were impressed with their serious attitude. No one said a word or uttered a sound. All walked through very slowly and inspected the numerous displays representing a portion of one of the most horrific acts of evil in human history. The children were coming to grips with the Holocaust. At Dachau, Marge and I also visited the Protestant Chapel, the Roman Catholic prayer chapel and a Synagogue. These were constructed after the war, as part of the Memorial at Dachau. Each was architecturally designed to express deep sorrow for the vast scope of the human tragedy represented at Dachau, as well as to express at least a glimmer of hope for the future. I wondered if those who designed the two Christian prayer Chapels were conscious of the silence and collaboration of Christian clergy before and during WW II.

I first learned of the problem of silence and collaboration of the clergy from my brother Roy, who learned of it at St. Olaf College.

Chapter 11

ROY RETURNS HOME FROM ST. OLAF COLLEGE: A TIME OF CONSCIENCE AND TORMENT

Roy completed his sophomore year at St. Olaf College in Northfield, Minnesota, in June, 1953. Roy was an excellent student and carried a double major in history and philosophy. He had also enrolled in ROTC and worked at the training very hard. Before his sophomore year Roy told me there were about 300 students enrolled in ROTC and he felt he was in the top 10. He had been an enthusiastic participant in ROTC, and he even thought about a career in the military. I have no doubt that his eagerness to learn about military training related to his memories of the Nazi occupation of Norway and the dangers of our escape. Memories such as the long days and nights aboard the MS Brant County in January, 1942 when the Norwegian captain Brevik made announcements of the ongoing wolf pack submarine attack on our convoy and the names of the ships that had been torpedoed and were sinking. Roy nourished thoughts that in a future war with the stakes of freedom on the one hand and terror on the other, he would fight for freedom.

Yet three days after Roy returned to our home in Muskegon, Michigan, in 1953, it was obvious that something was wrong. I did not understand what the matter was. Mom was distraught. She was angry, distressed and terribly disappointed. There was something about Roy or what he had done that changed her view of him. Mom argued with Roy and pleaded with him – but to no avail. Something about Roy that came from within had to change, but Roy would not change. Perhaps mom would have to accept and understand Roy as he now was, but she could not. Roy was tormented. He wondered if he had committed the sin that could not be forgiven. I had no idea of a sin that could not be forgiven, and yet Roy was tormented with the idea.

What had Roy done, I wondered? Why was our mother so upset with him? Why did dad pull out and disengage? I asked mom, "What's the matter with Roy?" She would not tell me. "It doesn't concern you," she said. I asked Roy what the matter was but weeks went by with increasing signs, words and gestures of concern and despair, but I did not understand what was wrong.

Finally, I said to Roy: "One day you must tell me what the matter is. You know what I mean, what is wrong? Why not tell me right now?"

Roy said he had had a complete change of view of war and was now opposed to war and would not fight. He had become a conscientious objector after a great personal struggle. He was still classified by the U.S. military as a regular potential draftee, and Roy had not yet scheduled a meeting with the draft board to change his status. He had told the senior officer of ROTC, who expressed a great deal of anger and tried to talk him out of becoming a conscientious objector. Roy withdrew from the ROTC after completing nearly all of the training.

Roy explained that when Ola Olsen came and spoke at St. Olaf College about the Norwegian resistance movement in which he played an important and courageous part, Roy for a considerable time afterwards had openings to talk about his own memories of the German occupation and our family's escape from German - occupied Norway. In a history class at St. Olaf, Roy spoke of the effort of Christians in Norway to resist the Nazi effort. He told of the pastoral letters condemning the Nazi oppression of the Jews, and the efforts, though only partially successful, to help Jews escape. Roy told of the clergy supporting the school teachers when they were under attack and pressured to sign an oath of support for the Nazi occupation of Norway. Roy conveyed the impression that resistance, as carried out under duress in Norway, had also taken place throughout occupied Europe.

The professor looked at Roy and shaking his head indicating "not so," said: "Roy, what you are saying is correct for both Norway and Denmark, but during WW II throughout occupied Europe, and in Germany, the Clergy were silent and did little or nothing to speak out against the Nazi terror and the Holocaust. Some actively collaborated."

At first Roy did not believe what he heard from his history professor. But his professor gave Roy extra reading assignments for him to learn a deeper background. Roy studied historical accounts of the intense pressure in Germany, after Hitler gained power in 1933, to turn the Christian church into a propaganda forum to support Nazi racist policy and anti-Semitism. Roy learned that Hitler appointed Ludwig Muller as Reich Bishop of the Protestant Church. Ludwig Muller moved quickly and force-fully to implement Nazi ideology to be the official stance of the Church.[1] By the summer of 1933 Deutsche Christian ("German Christian") implemented as church policy the "Aryan Paragraph" to prevent non-Aryans from becoming ministers or religious teachers. Even Jews who were "converted and baptized" were to be expelled from the Christian church. Furthermore, there was an effort to remove the Old Testament, and all things Jewish, from the Bible. [2]

Many church leaders in Germany, including those who were anti-Semitic, supported the "Judenmission" – the evangeliza-tion, conversion and baptism of Jews. This became prohibited because Jews could not under any circumstance be a member of a Christian church in Germany. This became official by a policy decision approved in September 1933 by the National Church Synod at Wittenberg.[3]

The Barmen Declaration of May 1934

A small but influential group of Christians in Germany – includ-ing Lutheran, and Reformed, and liberal and neo-orthodox met at

Barmen, Germany, and planned a strategy to resist the Nazi plan to twist the teachings of the Church for Nazi ends. They adopted a declaration written by Reformed theologian Karl Barth and Lutheran theologian Hans Asmussen. The declaration, known as the "Barmen Declaration," expressly rejected the claim that political influence such as from the Nazi regime had the authority to influence Church doctrine or its teachings.4 From this meeting at Barmen came the "Confessing Church." The Confessional Church declared itself to be the legitimate Protestant Church of Germany.

Unfortunately, there was considerable disunity among clergy who were members of the Confessing Church, which seriously weakened the impact of the movement. First, the "Barmen Confession" did not directly address the plight of Jews in Nazi Germany. While all members of the Confessing Church disagreed strongly with some aspects of the Nazification of the Protestant (Lutheran) Church in Germany, there was much dissent. Some members of the Confessing Church supported the broad aims of Adolf Hitler including its racist policy, and disagreed only on the issue about the new requirement that "converted and baptized Jews" were also to be expelled from the church. Other members of the Confessing Church were opposed to the persecution of Jews as a civil rights issue, and were eager to support Jews, including the vast majority who had no intention of converting to Christianity.

Pastor Martin Niemoller is an example of one who in the 1920's and 1930's held strong pro-Nazi and anti-Semitic views, which he freely preached from his pulpit. Martin Niemoller, the son of a Lutheran minister, was born in Lippstadt, Germany in 1892. During World War I he served as a captain on German submarines and under his command his submarines sank a number of British and French merchant ships, causing significant loss of life. He was awarded the Iron Cross, a major military honor in Germany. After the war Niemoller studied theology, was ordained as a Lutheran minister in 1929, and served as pastor of the Church of Jesus Christ at Dahlem, Germany. He supported Hitler and espoused Hitler's views on race and nationality.5 He published his autobiography, From U-Boat to Pulpit, which was endorsed by the Nazi press in Germany.6

In a sermon given in 1928, Niemoller referred to "...a curse on the Jewish people."

"It (the Jewish people) bears a curse, because it rejected Him and resisted Him to the death when it became clear that Jesus of Nazareth would not cease calling (the Jews) to repentance and faith..." 7

When the Nazi government denied civil rights to all Jews and, under directives from the Nazi Bishop, demanded that Jews be excluded from Christian churches, Niemoller joined with Dietrich Bonhoffer and formed the Pastors' Emergency League.8 He continued to focus on a "curse" for Jews who refused to convert. As late as 1935 he gave the following reason for the curse on Jews: "What is the reason for (their) obvious punishment, which has lasted for thousands of years: Dear brethren, the reason is easily given: the Jews brought the Christ of God to the cross!"9 Niemoller strongly resisted the Nazi policy that all Jews, including Jews who had converted to Christianity, were to be arrested. He was not otherwise opposed to the anti-Semitism of the Third Reich, for Jews who had not converted to Christianity. His view is a throwback to the period in Spain in 1492, when King Ferdinand ordered all Jews to leave Spain under the threat of death unless they converted to Christianity. 10

In a sermon he presented on Sunday, June 27, 1937, Niemoller gave specific examples of Nazi secret police arresting members of the Confessing Church in locations throughout Germany. His sermon was viewed as a violation against the State; consequently, Niemoller was arrested on July 1, 1937. His trial was delayed eight months and during that period he was incarcerated at the Moabit prison in Berlin. At his trial he was convicted of subversive acts against the State, fined and interned in Sachsenhausen and Dachau concentration camps from 1938 to 1945.11 Even while in prison he maintained some of his pro-Nazi views and sent a message in 1940 to the German Naval Commander asking if he could serve again as a captain of a German submarine.12 His offer was refused, and he continued to serve as a prisoner in Dachau. He was released by the allies in 1945. He underwent a spiritual transformation, renounced his earlier anti-Semitism, became a pacifist and in 1961 became president of the World Council of Churches. He is well known for his poem – "First they came …" 13 The poem presents a warning of the danger of silence in the face of evil.

First They Came

First they came for the communists
And I did not speak out
Because I was not a communist
Then they came for the Jews
And I did not speak out
Because I was not a Jew
Then they came for the trade Unionists
And I did not speak out
Because I was not a trade unionist
And then they came for me
And there was no one left
To speak out for me.

Pastor Niemoller (victim of the Nazis)

Dietrich Bonhoeffer was another church leader and minister, whose life and career were shaken and ripped by the Nazi take-over in Germany. He was born in Breslau, Germany, in 1906. His father was a professor of psychiatry and neurology. Bonhoeffer studied theology in Tubingen and in Berlin and completed a dissertation in 1927 and passed his theological exams in 1930. He traveled to the U.S. and studied at Union Seminary in New York under Reinhold Niebuhr. In 1931 Bonhoeffer returned to Germany and began teaching theology in Berlin.14

Bonhoeffer, like Niemoller, strongly objected to the Aryan Laws introduced by Hitler on April 7, 1933, to ban non–Aryans from civil service, from serving as ministers of a church or from having church membership. In direct response to the Aryan Laws Bonhoeffer prepared a document which he delivered for discussion to a group of pastors meeting at the home of Gerhard Jacobi in April 1933. This important document is called *The Church and the Jewish Question ((Die Kirche vor der Juden Frage)*. In his presentation he protested against any discrimination against Jews, without distinguishing between baptized and the nonbaptized Jew. He stated that the church must admonish the state (Hitler's Nazi Germany), and consider "jamming the spokes of the wheel," if the state continued to oppress the Jews.15 A number of pastors who were present objected to his presentation and left the meeting in protest. This is an early indication of a rift that cut through the Protestant pastors who came to represent the Confessing Church.

While Bonhoeffers remarks set him apart from many pastors who also opposed Nazism's attempt to bring the German churches in line with Hitler's policies, Bonhoeffer's words show that he had a long way to go to purge his theology from centuries of Christian anti-Semitism. Like Martin Niemoller, Bonhoeffer supported the "Judenmission," the evangelization, conversion and baptism of Jews to the Christian faith. He believed, like many Christians of his time, that Christianity had superceded Judaism. This concept was expressed by Bonhoeffer as follows: "The history of the suffering of this people, loved and punished by God, stands under the sign of the final homecoming of the people of Israel to its God, and this homecoming happens in the conversion of Israel to Christ."16

The Bethel Confession

By July 23, 1933, key leadership positions of the church were replaced by pro Nazi "Christians," as part of the rapidly developing and insidious Nazi takeover of the churches.. This was related to the "Jewish Question."17 In response Bonhoeffer and Professor

Hermann Sasse of Erlander were charged by a church council to produce a confession of faith to challenge the rapid inroads made by the German Christians. Bonhoeffer and Sasse retreated to the community of Bethel to produce a confession of faith. Their document clarified distinctions between the newly formed and avidly pro-Nazi "German Christians" versus the historic but now endangered German Evangelical Church. The document, which provided an uncompromising defense of the Jews, was sent to 20 pastors known to be disturbed by the extreme changes forced on the church since Hitler had come to power. However, the twenty pastors chipped away on the document and weakened it. Bonhoeffer then refused to sign the document (by then deeply compromised) that Martin Niemoller circulated. [18]

The Brown Synod

On September 4, 1933 a group of pro-Nazi clergymen met to establish as policy a number of pro-Nazi changes for the church in Germany. Many of these clergymen appeared in brown shirts, sporting the swastika, as a deliberate statement of support for Adolf Hitler. As a result the meeting became known as the Brown Synod of September 1933. These pro-Nazi clergymen succeeded in deposing an additional number of church leaders and replacing them with ten German Christian bishops sympathetic to Hitler. They also declared that the Aryan Clause was official church policy. [19] For Dietrich Bonhoeffer these changes meant that the church, i.e., "German Christian" of the Brown Synod was no longer a Christian Church. [20]

In response to actions taken by the Brown Synod, Bonhoffer, Niemoller and Franz Hilderbrandt met in mid September of 1933, at the home of the young pastor Gerhard Jacobi, to organize the Pastors' Emergency League. They declared that the decisions made by the Brown Synod were illegal and must be repealed and that the church must offer help to those victimized by the illegal and unjust laws. [21] They planned to raise their concerns at an up-coming meeting of church leaders, the National Synod scheduled to be held in the historic city of Wittenberg where, in the year 1517, Luther had posted his Ninety-Five Theses for debate when the issue of indulgences had provoked him to protest.

The National Synod at Wittenberg

Pro-Nazi bishop Ludwig Muller led the National Synod at Wittenberg in late September 1933. Bonhoeffer and Hildebrandt made repeated efforts to comment and bring to the floor the infamous church laws passed by the Brown Synod. Bishop Ludwig Muller absolutely refused their efforts to challenge the laws passed by the synod. In frustration Bonhoeffer and Hildebrandt nailed their protest letters to trees. 22 Bonhoeffer was distraught and he felt isolated. It was hard enough to tolerate the heretical changes to the Lutheran church brought on by the Nazi influence. In addition he was deeply troubled by disagreements within the emerging Confessional Church. He needed a break and he wrote to his friend Karl Barth, stating he wanted "to go into the wilderness for a spell." 23

Bonhoeffer left Germany and traveled to Chicheste, England, and continued to inform church leaders in Europe and North America, and Jewish leaders, about the growing threats in Europe related to Nazi Germany. While in England he assumed the pastorate of the German Evangelical Church, Sydenham, and the Reformed Church of St. Paul in London. Bonhoeffer began a strong friendship with Bishop George K. A. Bell of Chichester, England. He persuaded Bishop Bell to understand that the "German Christians" had become a tool of Nazism and their churches could not be considered Christian. He insisted that the Confessional Church should be recognized as the only true Protestant Christian church in Germany. 24

The Dahlem Synod of October 1934

In recognition of the increasing nazification of church policy, leaders of the Confessional Church met at the Dahlem Synod of

October 1934 to plan the building of seminaries to train clergy free of Nazi influence that had overtaken the German Church. Bonhoeffer agreed to direct the new seminary at Finkenwalde, near Stettin, in Pomerania. The Finkenwalde Seminary was organized to be true to the Gospel, the teachings of the Sermon on the Mount and for seminary students to develop a full understanding of church history during the middle ages that lead to the Reformation. In addition Dietrich Bonhoeffer advocated pacifism and conscientious objection to military service. The seminary opened in June 1935. 25

The Destruction of the Confessional Church

The historian William L. Shirer, in his account of the turmoil within the Protestant Church in Germany in the time span prior to and during WW II, has written that in the 1930's Germany had about 45,000,000 members of various subgroups of Lutheran and Reformed Churches. These were served by about seventeen thousand pastors. Of those pastors about three thousand clergymen were strongly supportive of the pro-Nazi "German Christian" belief system. He writes that about an equal number (about three thousand) were affiliated with the Confessional Church. 26

In response to the refusal of the Confessional Church leaders to accept the Nazi doctrine of Race, Blood and Soil, the Gestapo arrested 700 Confessional Church leaders in early 1935.27 Having failed to integrate the Confessional Church into the pro-Nazi "German Church," Reich Bishop Mueller resigned in July 1935. Hitler replaced him with Dr. Hans Kerrl as Minister for Church Affairs, with a directive to bring the members of the Confessional Church in line with the pro-Nazi German Church. In response Niemoller and other leaders of the Confessional Church sent a memo directly to Adolf Hitler protesting against State interference with the Church and denouncing the government for its anti-Semitism. This resulted in a severe attack against the Confessional Church; hundreds of Confessional Church leaders were arrested and Dr. Weissler, one of the signers of the memorandum was murdered. In addition, funds of the Confessional Church were confiscated and the Church was forbidden to accept collections. 28

It was in this context that Dr. Niemoiller was arrested on July 1, 1937; and later that year an additional 807 other pastors and leading laymen were arrested. In September 1937 the Seminary at Finkenwalde was closed by order of the Gestapo and many pastors and students were arrested. 29 Hundreds more clergy and leading laymen were arrested in the year 1938.

On April 20, 1938 all pastors in Germany were ordered to take the oath of allegiance to Adolf Hitler, including his racist policies. The vast majority of Protestant clergy complied, with the exception, of course, of the thousands who were in prison.

For Dietrich Bonhoeffer, the true Christian Protestant Church in Germany had ceased to exist. The editors Geffrey B. Kelly and F. Burton Nelson, in their book, *TESTAMENT TO FREEDOM: The Essential Writings of Dietrich Bonhoeffer*, state that Bonhoeffer was deeply distressed by the Nazi takeover in Germany, but even more distressed by the catastrophic failure of Christian leadership in Germany to stand up strong for the historic Church. Kelly and Nelson also state that the tactic - "Bonhoeffer had proposed was, in fact adopted by the Norwegian Church in the aftermath of actions against Provost Fjelibu and Bishop Berggrav. There followed a pastor's strike and wholesale church resignations." 30

Bonhoeffer continued to communicate with religious leaders throughout Europe and North America about the Nazi threat to Jews. As one example, he and his brother Klaus Bonhoeffer met with the American theologian Paul Lehmann and drafted a letter to U.S. Jewish leader Stephan Wise about the threat to Jews in Germany and in Europe. 31 Rabbi Wise later prepared a 20-page document about the threat to Jews in Europe under Nazi Germany and presented it to President Franklin Roosevelt.

In 1939 Hans von Dolnanyi, a lawyer married to Bonhoeffer's sister approached Bonhoeffer about joining him and others to resist the Nazi regime. The plan included an attempt to assassinate Adolf Hitler. Bonhoeffer's brother Klaus joined the effort.

Bonhoeffer was imprisoned in 1943 and executed in April 1945, just three weeks before the liberation of Germany. He maintained his faith to the end. 32

The degree to which Nazi influence penetrated the German Protestant churches is reflected by the following decree. Daniel Goldhagen writes: *In December 1941, Protestant Evangelical Church leaders of seven regions of Germany collectively issued an official proclamation that declared the Jews incapable of being saved by baptism, owing to their racial constitution; to be responsible for the war; and to be 'born enemies of the world and Germany.' They therefore urged that the 'severest measures against the Jews be adopted and that they be banished from German lands."* 33 Under these pressures ordinary citizens became pro-Nazi "Christians." The document also legitimized in the minds of Nazi authorities the requirement for clergy to provide the names of church members who had "converted" from Judaism to Christianity. In France and in other occupied countries, similar pressures were forced upon the church leaders and by and large the clergy gave in. 34

Information such as this was a shock to my brother Roy and to me as Roy discussed with me what he had learned from readings suggested by his college history professor. It was hard to believe the Nazis succeeded in suppressing the dissent advocated by leaders of the Confessing Church and that mainstream German churches by the end of 1937 held "Christian services" that supported and conveyed ruthless Nazi propaganda.

However, it was the awareness by Norwegian clergymen, in the 1930's, who traveled to Germany and saw first hand the Nazi effort to twist and distort the Christian message, that prepared them to fight tooth and nail against such pressures succeeding in Norway.

By 1942 Bishop Evind Berggrav was aware that Nazis were quoting the work of Martin Luther in Norway in their attempt to convince the Norwegian clergy to fully endorse Nazism as new era Christianity. In response Bishop Berggrav traveled throughout

Norway to persuade clergy not to be influenced by Nazi reference to Martin Luther whose writings were extremely anti-Semitic. Soon after these meetings, in the spring of 1942, Bishop Berggrav was imprisoned. Let us review some writings of Martin Luther that indeed anticipate Hitler.

Martin Luther and Anti-Semitism

Martin Luther was not a man of tolerance. The explosive rage of Martin Luther was directed at many sources and included Jews and poor peasants who protested against feudal lords.

Karen Armstrong writes: *"Luther was ... hostile to Jews. He told the Jews of Germany that, because he had reformed Christianity and made the Scriptures central, they could now become Christians: they would find their own Scriptures venerated, free of Romish error. This monstrous piece of impertinence showed absolutely no appreciation of the strong objection Jews have to the main Christian message. It arrogantly continued the old tradition of seeing Judaism as a mere prelude to and subsection of the "higher" religion of Christianity. When the Jews replied that they found a closer approximation to their Scriptures in the Talmud, Luther became aggressive. In his pamphlet, On the Jews and their Lies (1524) he looked forward to Hitler: Jews should be absolutely segregated from Christians, their homes must be demolished and they must live under one roof and do forced labor. Synagogues and prayer books should be burned. In 1517 Luther had already had the Jews expelled from Lutheran cities."* 35

Unfortunately, strong anti-Semitic views like that shown by Martin Luther were prevalent even among the German clergy who resisted Hitler and formed the Confessing Church. As stated above, this includes Martin Niemoller, who strongly resisted the Nazi policy that Jews who had converted to Christianity were also to be arrested and executed, but held on to serious aspects of anti-Semitism. While Niemoller was interned in Sachsenhausen concentration camp, he had discussions about Nazism with his cell mate. The cell mate, Leo Stein was released from Sachsenhausen and made it to America. Stein wrote an article about Neimoller for *The National Jewish Monthly*.36 Stein reported he asked Neimoller why he had supported the Nazi party, and Neimoller replied:

"I find myself wondering about that too. I wonder about it as much as I regret it. Still, it is true that Hitler betrayed me. I had an audience with him, as a representative of the Protestant Church, shortly before he became Chancellor, in 1932. Hitler promised me on his word of honor, to protect the Church, and not to issue any anti-Church laws. He also agreed not to allow pogroms against the Jews assuring me as follows: 'There will be restrictions against the Jews, but there will be no ghettos, no pogroms, in Germany.' Neimoller continued: "I really believed given the widespread anti-Semitism in Germany at the time – that Jews should avoid aspiring to government positions or seats in the Reichstag. There were many Jews, especially among the Zionists, who took a similar stand. Hitler's assurance satisfied me at the time. On the other hand, I hated the growing Atheistic movement, which was fostered and promoted by the Social Democrats and the Communists. Their hostility toward the Church made me pin my hopes on Hitler for a while. I am paying for that mistake now: and not just me, but thousands of other people like me."

Martin Luther and the Peasants' Revolt of 1525

Under the feudal system in Europe in the Middle Ages, the German peasantry, landless and long suffering from many impositions, formed a league, the *Bundschuh*, and turned to Luther for support. When conflict arose the peasants ransacked castles and monasteries. Apparently not fully appreciating the desperation of the peasants, Luther supported the establishment (feudal lords) against the peasants. He wrote a pamphlet, *Against the Murderous and Thieving Hordes of Peasants (1525)*, and urged violence against the peasants:

Therefore let everyone who can, smite, slay and stab, secretly or openly, remembering that nothing can be more poisonous, hurtful, or

*devilish than a rebel. It is just as when one must kill a mad dog, if you
don't strike him, he will strike you, and the whole land with you.* 37

In the violence and fighting that followed some five thousand
peasants were slain. Some were captured, tortured and beheaded.
In the 1930's and during WW II, German authorities used refer-
ences to Martin Luther to support both anti-Semitism and the
duty of Christians to be obedient to civil authority – and thus to
Nazi Germany.

The above information is a sample that is representative of
what Roy had learned during his sophomore year at St. Olaf. Roy
and mom had talked and argued about the information. Mom
could not accept that members of the Christian Church would
have done, or written, the things that Roy had talked about. She
tried to persuade Roy not to change his registration to that of
Conscientious Objector. Her argument was simply that in the
case of Nazi Germany, the only way to have defeated such an
evil government was through overwhelming military force. Roy
believed that if the Church had held to Christian values, the Nazi
government would never have gained power. Roy believed that it
was the failure of the Church to hold steadfast to the teachings of
Christ, and the ease with which the Nazis influenced the majority
of Christian clergy (Catholic and Protestant) that totally neutral-
ized the Church from being an effective fortress against the Hitler
regime. The failure is deep and as this chapter shows, the failure
goes back about one thousand years (dating back to 1095 when
Pope Urban made his famous crusade speech. The first large scale
pogrom against Jews came shortly after).

Roy agonized and pondered over these points during the
academic school year of 1953 – 1954. Rather than returning
to college he lived at home in Muskegon, Michigan, with our
family and drove a truck for a wholesale grocer and earned $1.00
per hour. He met with his draft board, who listened to his story
and without a problem they changed his draft status to that of

Conscientious Objector. After that troubled year was over, he was re-admitted to St Olaf and completed the last two years of his program of studies and graduated with honors.

He then served two years in the military stationed in Germany, and worked as a trained medic and ambulance driver. He was busy as a medic in responding to injuries that occurred to soldiers during military training and exercise, or injured in accidents off the base. He had high regard for the U.S. military, and enjoyed his chance to serve his country. After his military service, Roy earned a graduate degree from Michigan State University in history and philosophy and took a faculty position at Northern Michigan College in Traverse City, Michigan. He served there for over thirty years, and was highly regarded by students and other faculty. He married Margyl Eskedal in 1961 and they had three children. Roy died in April, 2006. Brother Edward and I attended a Memorial Service for him. I was impressed with the number of former students who attended the service. One student who drove many miles to attend told me after the service, "Roy was my best mentor. He is still my mentor."

Delayed Responses from Government and Church Officials: Unable to See and Unwilling to Acknowledge

Part of the agony and torment that Roy felt was his awareness that the Christian Church indeed had created an environment of hatred that contributed to some of the worst human tragedies of WW II. In the 1950's, just ten years after the war, almost no one agreed with Roy. Roy felt alone in his pain. He spoke with church pastors and leaders. Of about twenty, only one listened to Roy and shared his understanding of the dark side of church history. Roy felt guilty about his criticism of church leaders. He was greatly relieved after reading the works of the Danish exis-tentialist philosopher Soren Kirkegaard and his book, *Attack on Christendom*. Kirkegaard was a devout Christian, but he found deep flaws in how the Church went about its work and its drift from the message of Jesus Christ. Roy developed awareness that his own anguish was not with the message of Christ, but with the Christian Church – both Catholic and Protestant - that led generations of lay people on a path endorsing discrimination and oppression of some peoples.

Only recently have some government and Church officials of countries occupied by German forces begun to own up to their collaboration with the Nazis. Here are some examples given fifty plus years after WW II:

WALL OF NAMES MEMORIAL

In 1995, President Jacques Chirac of France acknowledged that France was responsible for systematically persecuting Jews during WW II, and that collaboration with the Nazis occurred among high government officials as well as ordinary citizens. One example of a high government official whose collaboration led to the deportation and death of large numbers of French Jews is that of Maurice Papon. During the war, Mr. Papon was an official of the Vichy government. In his government role the Germans asked him to arrest and deport Jews--and he complied. After the war, Mr. Papon managed to hide his past collaboration and he again assumed powerful positions in the French government. In 1998 after more than a decade of investigations of his Nazi collaboration, he was indicted of war crimes, tried and convicted. He served three years of a ten - year sentence, and died February 17, 2007.38

On January 27, 2005, President Chirac inaugurated the Wall of Names Memorial in Paris in memory of the 76,000 Jews rounded up with the collaboration of French people and sent to Nazi death camps. 39

Declaration of Repentance, issued by French Bishops in 1997.

In a remarkable move, French Bishops in 1997 issued the following Declaration of Repentance as a move towards reconciliation: "*It is a well-proven fact that for centuries, up until Vatican Council II, an anti-Jewish tradition stamped its mark in differing ways on Christian doctrine and teaching, in theology, apologetics, preaching and in the liturgy. It was on such grounds that the venomous plant of hatred for the Jews was able to flourish. Hence, the heavy inheritance we still bear in our century, with all its consequences which are so difficult to wipe out. Hence our still open wounds. To the extent that the pastors and those in authority in the Church let such a teaching of disdain develop for so long, along with an underlying basic religious culture among Christian communities which shaped and deformed people's attitudes, they bear a grave responsibility."* 40

Chapter 12

WHAT IF?

Writing after the war ended, Tore Gjelsvik, a leader in the Norwegian resistance movement, reflected on the worst scenario impacting Norway during WW II. He could have focused on the obliteration of the coastal community of Televag, or the loss of 4,500 Norwegian seamen and over 500 Norwegian ships engaged in the North Atlantic Convoy traffic, or the thousand plus Norwegian school teachers who were incarcerated at Kirkenes. He could have written about the numbers of his colleagues in the resistance movement who were captured, then either killed or tortured during interrogation sessions while in prison. Instead, he focused on the year 1942, and wrote the following:

The year was to end with the greatest blot on the entire history of Norway, namely the action of the Gestapo against the Norwegian Jews, who came to share the fate of their fellows on the continent through the march ... to annihilation in the gas chambers. The Home Front did what it could to help: the 'export' organizations used their capacity to the full - on the route from Oslo to Sweden it normally amounted to 50-60 persons per week – and new groups of 'exporters' were formed, made up of people who could not sit inactive and watch the violence done to these innocent victims. 1

Note that he did not limit the "worst scenario" to just the war period. He stated the violence done to Jews was the greatest blot "on the entire history of Norway." Let us dare to imagine a different scenario than the violence of the holocaust by imagining the question, "What if!" We must now look beyond Norway and take a look at broader Europe. Some readers will find this offensive. I will cover just a few examples.

Kristallacht

In 1938 on the anniversary of the birthday of the Martin Luther (born November 10, 1483) hundreds of Jewish Synagogues, Jewish businesses and homes were set aflame throughout Germany in what has been called Kristallnacht. What if German police and fire departments came to the rescue? That did happen once.

In Berlin the Neue Synagogue on Oranienburger Strasse was set ablaze by storm troopers. Wilhelm Krutzfeld, a German police superintendent, came immediately to the scene and put the area under police protection and ordered the fire department to put out the blaze. The blaze was extinguished, and the Neue Synagogue actually survived the war. Krutzfeld was threatened by Nazi officials and ordered to let the flames do their work. He refused and claimed that the building was a cultural monument. What if the action of Wilhelm Krutzfeld had been the response to the Kristallnacht throughout Germany? 2

Citizens Who Refused to Collaborate

What if, in occupied countries, citizens had refused to collaborate with Nazi authorities? French citizens collaborated with the German occupation force by submitting as many as 1,500 names of Jewish neighbors each week of their occupation, which made it possible for the German authorities to arrest and execute 76,000 French Jews.3 What if, instead of such collaboration, citizens of occupied countries provided shelter and protection for Jews?

This happened in the case of Paul Spiegel who was born on December 31, 1937. His family fled their home in Germany and crossed into Belgium. At risk to themselves a Christian family of farmers agreed to look after Paul and his mother. They survived the war. Unfortunately, Hugo Spiegel, the father of Paul Spiegel, was captured and endured five years in concentration camps at

Buchenwald, Auschwitz and Dachau. He was released at the end of the war. Then he learned that his neighbors had gone into ruins of the synagogue where he had worshiped and rescued Jewish sacred texts, protected them, and returned them when the Third Reich ended. Seeing what his neighbors had done, both to save his wife and his son as well as Jewish texts, Mr. Spiegel was convinced that Germany could still be home.4 What if this had been the norm?

Martin Gilbert, author of *Kristallnacht: Prelude to Destruction*, has written about a number of individuals who resisted the Nazi regime and assisted Jews to escape. Consider Pastor Heinrich Gruber, Dean of the Protestant Church in Berlin. He established a secret rescue operation in 1935 to organize escape routes to Holland. His organization became known as the 'Gruber Office,' by Jews who knew of it and managed to escape.

On the twenty-fifth anniversary of the outbreak of the Second World War, Henry Walter Brann, wrote of Pastor Heinrich Gruber; "The valiant churchman preached by day against Hitler's Jewish policies and operated escape routes for the Jews by night." 5

Another example given by Gilbert is that of Countess Maria von Maltzan, who had a brother in the Nazi SS. In spite of a family connection to the Nazi party, she contacted members of a Swedish Protestant Church in Berlin and helped large numbers of refugees to escape. 6

The Power of the Christian Press: For Good and Evil

The Bertelsmann publishing company in the 19th century was a Bible publisher. It also published religious literature for the Lutheran Church. What if this reputable company had resisted Nazism? It could have used its influence to print information questioning the racist policies of the Nazi regime, and defending the people oppressed in Germany as basic civil rights were taken away. However, Bertelsmann did not resist the Nazis, but used its ties with the Nazi regime to become a mass-marketing publisher and the largest supplier of books to the German army. Many of the books were clearly anti-Semitic. Bertelsmann continued to print religious literature; however, the anti-Semitic tone of its religious writing was even more pronounced and included Nazi terminology. Furthermore, during the war the company used Jewish slave labor at some of its printing plants.

In 1998 Thomas Middelhoff, then chairman of Bertelsmann, gave an address in New York. He asserted that the company had not collaborated with the Nazi regime, and instead was shut down in 1944 because it had published books banned by the Nazis. His address prompted a strong refutation bay Hersch Fischler who published articles revealing the Nazi collaboration of Bertelsmann during the war in a Swiss magazine, *Die Weltwoche,* and in *The Nation.*7

To its credit Bertelsmann appointed in 1998 an independent commission to investigate the company's wartime history. In 2002 the scholars produced a 794-page report, specifying the nature and extent of the company's Nazi collaboration and efforts to cover it up. On October 7, 1998, the company acknowledged the report and expressed regret for its Nazi era conduct. Bertelsmann has made amends and has joined 6,000 German companies who have agreed to pay $4.5 billion dollars in reparations.8

Our Judeo-Christian Heritage: A Brief Look Back

What if church leaders, both Protestant and Catholic, acknowledge centuries of anti-Semitism within Christendom and begin to collaborate towards reconciliation?

What if Pope Urban II, in the year 1095, had urged European Christians to travel to the Holy Land in peace, rather than as violent warriors? Instead, tens of thousands of Muslims met their death in the Middle East during the two-hundred year period of the Crusades. Furthermore, the first wide spread pogrom against Jews in Europe occurred shortly after the Pope called for the First Crusade. 9 Our world is still profoundly impacted by the historical events of the Crusades.

What if Pope Alexander VI had spoken out against the order

given by the King of Spain in 1492 that Jews and Muslims must leave Spain or face execution unless they converted to Catholicism? Receiving no support 60,000 Jews escaped to Portugal. For a few years the Jews prospered, but then King Manuel I of Portugal imposed a variation of the same threat. The Jews must convert to Catholicism or leave Portugal, or risk being burned at the stake. Many fled to Eastern Europe; others endured humiliating public baptisms and were designated "New Christians" or the offensive Iberian slang "Marranos." In 1506, about 3,000 Jews were massacred in Lisbon, Portugal in a religious riot. 10

What if Martin Luther, back in 1531, had looked beyond his own prejudice and animosity, reconciled with the Jewish people and not espoused virulent anti-Semitism?

What if Protestant clergy today were open and forthright with their congregations about the long history of anti-Semitism, loudly proclaimed from the very beginning of the Protestant Reformation: What if Roman Catholics could participate in honest and open discussions of the history of anti-Semitism within the Catholic Church: The long history of anti-Semitism within the Christian church contributed to both the silence and to the collaboration so necessary for the Nazi agenda to accomplish its lethal work.

What if the outstanding work of the Second Vatican Council, which denounced anti-Semitism, had taken place two decades or more before WW II, rather than more than two decades after the war?

What if Pope Pius XII had Denounced Nazism?

Daniel Goldhagen, in his book *A Moral Reckoning: The Role of the Catholic Church in the Holocaust and its Unfulfilled Duty of Repair*, asks the question:

Imagine that Pius XII had instructed every bishop and priest across Europe, including in Germany, to declare in 1941 that the Jews are innocent human beings deserving, by divine right, every protection that their countrymen enjoyed, and that anti-Semitism is wrong, and that killing Jews is an unsurpassable transgression and mortal sin, and that any Catholic contributing to their mass murder would be excommunicated and would surely have to answer for his deeds in the next world. Imagine that Pius XII had broadcast the same declaration over Vatican Radio and the BBC throughout Europe had printed it on their front pages. Imagine that Pius XII and all European clergy, including German clergy, had then decreed it a moral duty for all Europeans to resist this evil. Does anyone really believe that many more Jews would not have been saved? 11

The Meaning of the Churches' Role in WW II for Brothers Roy, Edward and Leif.

Roy was deeply affected by what he learned about the extent of the collaboration by church leaders, government officials in Nazi-occupied countries and leaders of industry. As stated in chapter 11, Roy was painfully introduced to the culpability of the Christian Church for its long history of anti-Semitism, when Roy naively stated in his college history class that Christians in Europe helped save many Jews. The professor who was familiar with our family's story of escape corrected Roy and said, "I understand the people of Denmark and Norway helped save many Jews and the church helped, but that is not true for the Church in Germany or in the other occupied countries."

After several months of extra (non-credit) reading assignments, Roy recognized that his view of the world had to be turned upside down. It was a stressful and life changing period for him. In the late 1940s and early 1950's, Germany was to take full responsibility for the Holocaust, with almost no reference to collaboration from outside the Nazi party. Only within the past decade or so have some leaders of State publicly acknowledged, with regret, wide spread collaboration: President Jacque Chirac of France in 1995, Bishops of the French Catholic Church in 1997, and major industrial organizations, such as Bertelsmann in Gutersloh, Germany, (now one of the world's largest media conglomerates with over 76,000 employees) in 2002.

Some immediate changes that Roy made include his change of a career goal from military service to a career in teaching, and the change of his draft status to that of Conscientious Objector. After completing his military service and graduate-level education, Roy joined the faculty at Northern Michigan College, in Traverse City, Michigan. As a faculty member he did not harangue students to his point of view, nor did he focus on WW II. He stressed the importance of questioning, and encouraged his students to gather background information on controversial topics. He often told his students, : "Question everything, research the issues, and then tell me what you think!"

Edward was fourteen months old when we left Norway on the "Shetland Bus," *Siglaos,* and seventeen months old when we arrived in New York City. Edward says he has no memory of our escape. However, the events in Norway during the occupation and of our escape were frequent topics of conversation within our family. This was especially true when the war ended and we were then able to correspond with relatives in Norway. Discussions increased again when Roy took a year off from college to ponder the war and the ethical and moral issues of the role of the Church in what it did do and in what it failed to do.

Edward took all this information into consideration. He was a good student and after graduating from college he attended Michigan State University and received a Masters degree in physics and math, and a graduate degree in media. Edward took a position as a high school math and science teacher at a U.S. military base in Japan and held that position for two years. He became persuaded that U. S. government foreign policy was excessively militarily oriented, and was focused to protect U.S. economic interests in foreign affairs over peace and justice. He was particularly concerned about U.S. policies in Central America. This led him to become active in well organized peaceful demonstrations. He also viewed as dangerous, the excess in nuclear weapons-development in the United States.

In 1982 Edward joined a broad based group of peaceful

demonstrators to protest the establishment of a large nuclear submarine base on Hood Canal, Washington, with submarines carrying nuclear tipped warheads. I will elaborate on this, as but one example, of his efforts as a peaceful protestor.

Early in 1982 the U.S. Navy disclosed that the nation's first Trident submarine would arrive on its maiden voyage to the Naval Submarine Base Bangor on Hood Canal. The U.S. government gave no announcement of the specific arrival date. However, concerned citizens who were prepared to demonstrate and protest began to arrive in Port Townsend, Washington, from all parts of the country and from overseas. By early August anticipation of the arrival of the Trident submarine, the *USS Ohio*, was heightened by a series of government announcements. For example, on the weekend of August 7 and 8, the Federal Aviation Administration closed airspace over Hood Canal. In addition, the U.S. Coast Guard closed two Coast Guard Stations along the Oregon Coast and sent dozens of Coast Guard Ships to the area of Hood Canal.

Waiting for the arrival of the Trident was a large group of protestors and about 20 boats. The largest was a 54-sailboat, *Pacific Peacemaker*, which had sailed from Australia. Another was the 48-foot sailboat the *Lizard of Woz*. My brother, who used to commercial salmon troll with me on the Oregon coast, was to be the "captain" of a 16 foot aluminum boat with an outboard motor – the smallest "ship" in the armada of protestors.

William A. Ethel, captain of the *Pacific Peacemaker*, told Alan K. Ota, a reporter for The Oregonian, his boats six months journey from Australia was sponsored by Australian religious and labor groups. He stated that it was the hope of the demonstrators that some of the more than twenty boats would be able to elude the large flotilla of Coast Guard escort boats and circle the *USS Ohio* Trident submarine. Other demonstrators included Charles Mesconis, leader of a peace task force for the Seattle Council of Churches, Pat Herron, a member of the environmental group Greenpeace, and Ruth Youngdahl Nelson, age 78, a former American "Mother of the Year" from Minnesota.

On Thursday, August 12, 1982, the nation's Trident Submarine, the *USS Ohio*, made its long-awaited appearance into Admiralty Inlet escorted by nine Coast Guard ships. The crew of the *USS Ohio* bore witness to a spectacular scene as several dozen Coast Guard boats sprayed protestors with high-pressure water hoses and ousted them from the boats that were attempting to surround the submarine. The Coast Guard personnel, armed with automatic weapons boarded the *Pacific Peacemaker* and the *Lizard of Woz*, handcuffing the crews and protestors. As the submarine passed by, most of the protestors, in handcuffs, watched while in custody from more than a mile away.

My brother Edward remained on his 16-foot outboard powered aluminum boat accompanied by two-fellow protestors. They were ignored by the Coast Guard who focused on the larger vessels. *The Oregonian* reported a dramatic and unexpected turn of events as follows:

When the submarine finally passed with an escort of nine Coast Guard boats, most of the protestors watched in handcuffs from more than a mile away at the western edge of the channel.

However, one small aluminum motorboat, occupied by three protest-ers, suddenly eluded the Coast Guard net and shot through the escort surrounding the USS Ohio. It came to within a short distance of the submarine.

Lou Parris, a Coast Guard photographer who watched from a helicopter, said the boat, piloted by Edward Terdal, 42, of Ashland, Ore. 'got within 75 yards of the submarine' and circled around 'in front of it' before being chased down by two patrol boats and a helicopter. Other occupants of the boat were Renee Krisko, 40, of Poulsbo, Wash., and Sunshine Appleby of Bolinas, Calif.

Other Resistance Activities by Edward

Edward once joined a group of peaceful demonstrators who traveled to Nicaragua to show support for its citizens. A main goal was to show them that many citizens of the U.S. seeks friendly terms with citizens of Nicaragua, and do not share the values of the United States' military interventions in Central America that support dictatorships who in turn support economic interests of U.S. industry.

Edward eventually shifted his focus. He told me that rather than protest "evil," he would intervene by helping people who for one reason or another were downtrodden. He spent a year as a volunteer sheepherder in Arizona, during a time when the United States government attempted to intervene between land conflicts concerning Native American Hopi Indians and Navaho. He felt the Native American groups could resolve their problems better without U.S. government intervention.

He then shifted his residence to Port Townsend, Washington. With the collaborative help of seven Protestant Churches, Edward served as a volunteer house parent for a group of homeless men, who had a history of un-employment and minor run-ins with the law. Edward established some basic rules for the residence such as no alcohol or drug use, and non-violence. He patiently taught the residents to share work responsibilities within the home; and he assisted some of the men to get low-level employment. He managed this effort for about seven years.

Edward married in 1996. He and his wife Elaine now live in the Puget Sound area, and Edward is using his academic background as a full time high school science teacher.

Edward has drawn insights from the Norwegian resistance movement of WW II. While occupied by an overpowering German army, Norwegians were effective in using non-violent strategies to influence change. The resistance shown by the clergy of the Norwegian Lutheran Church, and by thousands of school teachers was simply, "We will not endorse, nor will we carry out acts that are against our conscience. Furthermore, we will speak out against Nazi attempts to influence the culture, laws and ideals of Norwegian society." This certainly included the Nazi-German persecution of Jews in Norway. When Nazi actions violated Norwegian laws, the Clergy reminded fellow Norwegians, "If we remain silent, we are collaborators!"

Note: I am not assuming that you will agree with all, or even any, of the causes that Edward spent so much time and effort to punctuate and oppose. I simply wanted to show Edward's take as a citizen about some United States policies that contradicted our own nation's values. His non-violent protests were based in part on his understanding of the Norwegian experience in World War II.

Some Personal Reflections

As I reflect on the impact of the war, the terms of the occupation and of our escape from Norway, I am strongly influenced by how Norwegian church leaders, educators, business people and the citizens responded to the military defeat and the occupation. This provides me with a template to reflect on some difficult issues within the United States.

Consider the Stated Rationale for War

When a head of state initiates an attack on another country, the stated reason for war may not be the real reason. When Germany attacked Norway in 1940, Norwegians were told the German government has "offered their assistance to the government of Norway." Germany had sent its military to "protect" Norway from England. We know the stated reason for the attack was different in part because German archives clearly state the reasons for the invasion and the time-frame for when the invasion was to occur. In the case of the United States invasion of Iraq, the stated reasons were "to locate and destroy weapons of mass destruction," and to search out and eliminate the link between Saddam Hussein and al Qaeda. The stated reasons were a cover, that is, a rationale for the war, but not the reasons.

Other Lessons that Apply to the United States

1. Military Power is Overrated
Germany employed over 350,000 troops in their attack on Norway, and Germany won the military phase of the war. Then what?

Germany was unable to influence more than a small minority of
Norwegians (about two percent) to collaborate with the Nazi occupation. Germany was unable to establish a Vichy-type regime
in Norway, as they had in occupied France. In the case of the
United States invasion of Iraq, the United States has employed
about 160,000 troops in a country of about 22, 000,000. If the
United States were to have the same proportion of troops in Iraq,
as Germany had in Norway (population 3,000,000 in 1940), the
number of U.S. troops would have to be increased to a level of
two and one half million troops. Then what? The United States
probably still could not influence the various sectors of the Iraq
society to establish a government that suited the United States.
This point has been addressed. For example, former President
George H.W. Bush and Brent Scowcroft explained in 1998
why they had not gone into Bagdad in 1991: "Had we gone the
invasion route, the United States could conceivably still be an occupying power in a bitterly hostile land." (NYT 12/11/2006).

2. The Power of Non-Violence is Underrated

Non-violent resistance can be effective, even under conditions
of an occupying power with an overwhelming military force.
Consider again the case of the Norwegian church. If one pastor out of six had decided to take a strong position against the
Nazi occupation forces, the German forces in Norway might
well have arrested and executed all of them. However, when the
proportion of resistors was near 95 percent, the Germans limited
their response to occasional imprisonments and executions. The
remaining clergy in Norway were free to influence Norwegian
opinion very effectively, even though their churches were shut
down by the Nazis. This is in marked contrast to the situation
in Germany where only 3,000 Protestant pastors resisted the
Nazi ideology, and about 14,000 pastors signed an agreement to
support the ideology of Hitler. With that comparatively weak
resistance (about one pastor out of six), Adolf Hitler was able to
arrest the resistant Protestant clergy (members of the Confessing

Church) and imprison and execute them at will. In Norway well over 90 percent of school teachers resisted the Nazi-occupation demands; that was not the case in Germany.

3. Protestantism in the United States Today: Similarities with the "German Christian" Church.

Let us consider a range of issues in which current Protestant church leaders depart from traditional Christian values and support neo-conservative militaristic agendas. We start with the issue of Torture.

In March 2007 seventeen prominent Protestant evangelical leaders issued,

An Evangelical Declaration against Torture: Protecting Human Rights in an age of Terror

The declaration had been prepared by David P. Gushee, chair of HER (Evangelicals for Human Rights), and a professor of moral philosophy at Union University.

The document reads in part,

"We renounce the resort to torture and cruel, inhuman and degrading treatment of detainees, call for the extension of procedural protections and human rights to all detainees, seek clear government-wide embrace of the Geneva Conventions, including those articles banning torture and cruel treatment of prisoners, and urge the reversal of any U.S. government law, policy or practice that violates the moral standards outlined in this declaration." (the web site for the declaration is www.evangelicalsforhumanrights.org.)

Religious conservatives immediately found fault with the document and were quick to dismiss it. Mark D. Tooley, of the neo-conservative Institute on Religion and Democracy muted the document by declaring it as the work of "pseudo-pacifist academics and antiwar activists" who were contributing to "a barely disguised crusade against the U.S. war against terror." Daniel R. Heimbach, a Southern Baptist professor of ethics at Southwestern

Baptist Theological Seminary labeled the declaration as a "diatribe." (NYT 7/21/2007).

My personal concern about torture relate in part to our family's experience in Norway during the war. The two men who did the most to arrange for us to escape, Mr. Ola Olsen and Dr. Sigurd Hus, were both subjected to torture. Aside from physical beatings, Mr. Olsen was subjected to being told by one of the guards, "Mr. Olsen we have captured your son! We will execute him if you do not respond to our questions!" Mr. Olsen replied, "Kill me, not my son, but I will tell you nothing!" (Dietrich Bonhoeffer endured a similar threat and outcome, i.e., death to members of his family unless he revealed information to Nazi interviewers.) Dr. Sigurd Hus died after the war of injuries he received while enduring punitive interview strategies.

Perhaps Mark D. Tooley and Daniel R. Heimbach, who casually dismissed the issue of torture, are unfamiliar with information suggesting that torture may remain U.S. policy in our war against Iraq and Afghanistan. Here is a brief background.

The Abu Ghraib Prison

The order for the 320th Military Police Battalion to be sent to Iraq came on February 5, 2003. Few of the 1,000 members had been trained to guard enemy prisoners. These soldiers were destined to be in charge of Abu Ghraib during a time of increasing rage of anti-American insurgency and coupled with American commanders being desperate for information about the insurgency.

By May 1, 2003 came the declaration that major combat operations had ended. However, the insurgency against the U.S. occupation continued to increase. At this time the 320th Military Police Battalion was guarding a large barbed wire prison camp in the desert known as Camp Bucca. Soon Camp Bucca was at overcapacity. The army chose Abu Ghraib as the new American prison. The prison was well known throughout Iraq as the prison where Saddam Hussein had ordered execution and acts of torture against persons who were accused of opposing him. In July 2003 the 320th Battalion was sent to run the world's largest prison operated by the United States Army. Within a short period of time, the prison at Abu Ghraib had over 7000 prisoners.

By 2004 compelling information revealed that prisoners at Abu Ghraib had been tortured, sexually abused and humiliated, stripped, shackled and beaten. Much of the information was filmed by the U.S. guards in charge of Abu Ghraib. People imprisoned were not offered even the semblance of due process. They were not charged; they had no access to lawyers, and were not given the right to appeal.

The U.S. army has investigated G.I. prison abuse, and in a document dated May 5, 2004, report that abuse is more wide spread than previously suspected and included other military units in addition to the 320th Battalion. The abuses specified in the army document indicated that some prisoners were killed while in custody. (NYT May 26, 2004). The United States Military also report that 70 to 90 percent of the people detained in Iraq had been seized by mistake. (NYT March 28, 2005).

Specialist Sabrina Harman, of the 372nd, was interviewed by Errol Morris about the abuses at Abu Ghraib. One of her statements referred to the practice of taking young children as prisoners in an effort to capture or break the child's father. She referred to one prisoner as a ten year old, and stated – "It was kind of sad that they even had to be there." In reference to the ten year old, Morris reports that Sabrina Harman continued - "…a little kid, he could have fit through the bars, he was so little." (Philip Gourevitch, Errol Morris, *Exposure: Behind the cameras at Abu Ghraib,* in The New Yorker, March 24, 2008.) Gourevitch and Morris, state,

Yet, the abuse of prisoners at Abu Ghraib was de facto United States policy. The authorization of torture and the decriminalization of cruel, inhuman, and degrading treatment of captives in wartime have been among the defining legacies of the current Administration; and the rules of interrogation that produced the abuses documented on the M.I. block in the fall of 2003 were the direct expression of the hostility toward international law and military doctrine that was found in the White House, the Vice-President's office, and the highest levels of the Justice and Defense Departments. (page 49)

Is Torture O.K.?

Dr. John C, Green has conducted an analysis of poling data on attitudes towards torture and terrorism by the Pew Research Center during the years 2004, 2005 and 2006. In most religious groups those who worshipped weekly were most likely to be restrictive and state that torture should not be used. The exception was that white, protestant evangelicals were more likely to approve of the use of torture; these weekly worshippers "tend to be more Republican, conservative and supportive of the Bush administration than their co-religionists."

American Protestant Evangelicals: Some Positions on Israel and Palestine

On July 27, 2007 a coalition of 34 evangelical leaders sent a letter to President Bush urging him to take a more even stance on the Israeli-Palestinian situation in the Middle East. The letter stated that both Israelis and Palestinians have "legitimate rights stretching back for millennia to the lands of Israel/Palestine." The evangelical leaders included in their letter support for the creation of a Palestinian state to include the majority of the West Bank, and they stated that being a friend and supporter of Israel does not mean, "withholding criticism when it is warranted."

The signers include Gary M. Benedict, president of the Christian and Missionary Alliance, a denomination of 2,000 churches, Richard J. Mouw, a president of Fuller Theological Seminary; Gordon Mac Donald, chairman of World Relief; Richard E. Stearns, president of World Vision; David Neff, editor of Christianity Today; and Berten A. Waggoner, national director and president of The Vineyard USA, an association of 630 churches in the United States. (NYT 7/29/2007).

The Rev. John Hagee Launches a Diatribe

The Rev. John Hagee was shown the letter and responded as follows:

Bible-believing evangelicals will scoff at the message.

Christians United for Israel is opposed to America pressuring Israel to give up more land to anyone for any reason. What has the policy of appeasement ever produced for Israel that was beneficial?

God gave to Abraham, Isaac and Jacob a covenant in the Book of Genesis for the land of Israel that is eternal and unbreakable, and that covenant is still intact. The Palestinian people have never owned the land of Israel, never existed as an autonomous society. There is no Palestinian language. There is no Palestinian currency. And to say that Palestinians have a right to that land historically is an historical fraud.

What are the Real Tenants of the Evangelical Faith?

Gordon MacDonald, one of the signers of the letter to President Bush urging a balanced stance on the Israeli-Palestinian situation in the Middle East, has expressed profound dismay at the response given by Rev. Hagee:

My own sense is that the NAE (as we know it) will probably not recover from this awful moment. Ever since the beginning of the Bush Administration, I have worried...we are part of an evangelical movement that is greatly compromised-identified in the eyes of the public as deep in the hip pockets of the Republican party and administration. My own belief? Our movement has been used. Like it or not, we area pictured as those who support war, torture, and a go-it-alone (bullying) posture in international relationships. Any of us who travel internationally have tasted the global hostility toward our government and the suspicion our President's policies reflect the real tenants of the Evangelical Faith.

As I reflect on my families escape from Norway, and the strong and united resistance demonstrated by Norwegians against Nazism, I am greatly concerned with a contradiction. The contradiction is seen in the growing political influence of people like the San Antonio mega-church pastor John Hagee. He advocates war-like positions in the name of Christianity. He is lobbying Washington to consider a pre-emptive U.S. military strike against Iran-ostensibly to protect Israel. Politicians like John McCain, Newt Gingrich, Joe Lieberman and President George W. Bush have sought his endorsement. Some have appeared with him on his stage in front of crowds of enthusiasts.

I see a comparison between Pastor John Hagee and the large majority of Protestant clergy in Germany in the 1930's and during the war years, who fell over themselves to be in alignment with the "powers that be." The extreme bias advocated by Pastor John John Hagee is dangerous. It is inappropriate to use Old Testament Scripture written thousands of years ago to eliminate any regard for the rights, values and needs of the Palestinians in today's world.

During the past sixty years, Christianity has not survived very well in Europe. This is reflected in markedly diminished church attendance, which I believe stems in part from the failure of the church to maintain and exemplify just and ethical values in the lead up to and during WW II. There may be a lesson for us. Are we paying attention?

ENDNOTES

CHAPTER ONE

1. The La Follette-Furuseth Law of 1915 made it easy for Scandinavian sailors, drawn by higher wages in the American Merchant Marine, to desert their vessels in New York. In the fifteen-year period from 1876 to 1890, 19,487 Norwegian seamen stepped ashore in America and sought work with American shipping. The La Follette-Furuseth Law of March 1915 made "jumping ship" legal. No seamen could be arrested by the police and brought back on board. Reference: A.N. Rygg, *Norwegians In New York: 1825-1925*. (The Norwegian News Company, Brooklyn, N.Y., 1941), p. 25.

2. Gilbert, Martin, *KRISTALLNACHT: Prelude to Destruction*. (New York: Harper Collins *Publishers*, 2006).

3. Jurgen Rohwer, *War At Sea 1939-1945*. (Chatham Publishing, an imprint of Gerald Duckworth & Co Ltd. 2001), pp.19-29.

4. Francois Kersaudy, *Norway 1940*. (Lincoln: University of Nebraska Press, 1987), p. 44.

5. Florence Jaffray Harriman, *Mission to the North*. (New York: J. B. Lippincott Company, 1941), p. 247-248.

6. Kersaudy, *Norway 1940, op. cit.*, pp. 38-47.

7. Kersaudy, *Norway 1940, op. cit.*, pp. 9-12.

8. Harriman, *Mission to the North, op. cit.*, pp. 92-95.

9. Harriman, *Mission to the North, op. cit.*, p. 57.

10. Ronald G. Popperwell, *Norway: Nation of the Modern World*. (London: Ernst Benn Limited Bouverie House, 1972), pp. 94-95, 192, 218.

11. Popperwell, *Norway: Nation of the Modern World, op. cit.*, p. 118.

12. Popperwell, *Norway: Nation of the Modern World, op. cit.*, pp. 282-285.

13. Kersaudy, *Norway 1940, op. cit.*, p.58.

14. Kersaudy, *Norway 1940, op. cit.*, p.62.

CHAPTER TWO

1. Kersuady, *Norway 1940, op. cit., p. 48.*
2. Kersuady, *Norway 1940, op. cit., p.48.*
3. Kersuady, *Norway 1940, op. cit., p.47.*
4. Kersuady, *Norway 1940, op. cit., p.* 71
5. Kersuady, *Norway 1940, op. cit.,* p. 69
6. Kersuady, *Norway 1940, op. cit.,* p. 71
7. Kersuady, *Norway 1940, op. cit.,* p. 72
8. Olav Riste and Berit Nokleby, *NORWAY 1940–45: THE RESISTANCE MOVEMENT.* (Aschehoug: Printed in Norway by Nor-Media A/S, 1970).
9. Kersuady, *Norway 1940, op. cit.,* p. 78-79.
10. Kersuady, *Norway 1940, op. cit.,* p. 67-72.
11. Kersuady, *Norway 1940, op. cit.,* p. 96.
12. Kersuady, *Norway 1940, op. cit.,* p. 103.
13. Kersuady, *Norway 1940, op. cit.,* pp. 103-105.
14. Kersuady, *Norway 1940, op. cit.,* pp. 103-104.
15. Kersuady, *Norway 1940, op. cit.,* p. 105.
16. Kersuady, *Norway 1940, op. cit.,* pp. 105-106.
17. Kersuady, *Norway 1940, op. cit.,* pp. 122-123.
18. Kersuady, *Norway 1940, op. cit.,* pp. 123-128.
19. Kersuady, *Norway 1940 ,op. cit.,* pp. 129-130.
20. Kersuady, *Norway 1940, op. cit.,* pp. 179-181
21. Kersuady, *Norway 1940, op. cit.,* p. 156
22. Kersuady, *Norway 1940, op. cit.,* p. 169
23. Kersuady, *Norway 1940, op. cit.,* p. 169
24. Kersuady, *Norway 1940, op. cit.,* p. 170
25. Kersuady, *Norway 1940, op. cit.,* p. 172
26. Kersuady, *Norway 1940, op. cit.,* p. 181
27. Kersuady, *Norway 1940, op. cit.,* p. 147

CHAPTER THREE

1. Harriet Terdal, *Our Escape From Nazi-Occupied Norway,* (Self published manuscript, 1971), p. 3.
2. FO 371/23659, Intelligence Department of Ministry of Economic Warfare, 27/11/1939. Cited in Francois Kersuady, *Norway, 1940,* p. 17.
3. Kersuady, *Norway 1940,* p. 122.

4. Kersuady, *Norway 1940,* p. 125.
5. Kersuady, *Norway 1940,* p. 127.
6. Kersuady, *Norway 1940,* p. 127.
7. Kersuady, *Norway 1940,* p. 145.
8. Kersuady, *Norway 1940,* p. 158.
9. Kersuady, *Norway 1940,* p. 195.
10. Kersuady, *Norway 1940,* p. 197.
11. Kersuady, *Norway 1940,* p. 200.
12. Kersuady, *Norway 1940,* p. 218.
13. Kersuady, *Norway 1940,* p. 216.
14. Kersuady, *Norway 1940,* p. 218.
15. Kersuady, *Norway 1940,* p. 219.
16. Kersuady, *Norway 1940,* p. 223.

CHAPTER FOUR

1. Harriet Terdal, *Our Escape From Nazi-Occupied Norway,* (Self published manuscript, 1971), and presented in its entirety as Chapter Seven.

CHAPTER FIVE

1. Hoye, Bjarne and Trygve M. Ager, *The Fight of the Norwegian Church Against Nazism.* (New York: The Macmillan Company, 1943)., p.9.
2. Hoye, Bjarne and Trygve M. Ager, *The Fight of the Norwegian Church Against Nazism, op. cit.* p. 17.
3. *Ibid.,* p. 18.
4. *Ibid.,* p. 22.
5. *Riste and Nokleby, Norway 1940-45: The Resistance Movement, op. cit.* p. 20.
6. Hoye, Bjarne and Trygve M. Ager, *The Fight of the Norwegian Church Against Nazism, op. cit., p. 23.*
7. *Ibid., p.* 15.
8. *Ibid., p.* 7.
9. *Ibid., pp. 21-39.*
10. *Riste and Nokleby, Norway 1940-45: The Resistance Movement, op. cit., p. 24.*
11. Hoye, Bjarne and Trygve M. Ager, *The Fight of the Norwegian Church Against Nazism, op. cit.,* p. 29.

12. *Ibid.,* p. 32.
13. Mendelsohn, Oskar, *The Persecution of the Norwegian Jews in WW II.* (Norges Hjemmefrontmuseum, 2000). pp. 8-10.
14. *Ibid.,* p. 9.
15. Hoye, Bjarne and Trygve M. Ager, *The Fight of the Norwegian Church Against Nazism, op. cit.,* p. 62.
16. *Ibid.,* p. 18.
17. *Ibid.,* p. 62.
18. *Ibid.,* p. 63.
19. *Ibid.,* p. 65.
20. *Ibid.,* p. 66.
21. *Ibid.,* pp. 70-75.
22. *Ibid.,* pp. 75-79.
23. *Ibid.,* pp. 93-106.
24. Mendelsohn, Oscar, *The Persecution of the Norwegian Jews in WW II, op. cit.,* p. 15.
25. *Ibid.,* p. 18.
26. *Ibid.,* p. 11.
27. *Ibid.,* p. 10.
28. *Ibid.,* p. 7
29. *Ibid.,* p. 29
30. Riste and Nokleby, *Norway 1940-45: The Resistance Movement, op. cit.,* p. 44.
31. Mendelsohn, Oskar, *The Persecution of the Norwegian Jews in WW II, op. cit.,* p. 11.
32. *Ibid.,* p. 11.
33. Ousby, Ian, *Occupation: The Ordeal of France: 1940-1944,* New York: St. Martin's Press, 1998, p. 179.
34. Mendelsohn, Oskar, *The Persecution of Norwegian Jews in WW II, op. cit.,* p.15.
35. *Ibid.,* p. 17.
36. *Ibid.,* p. 22.
37. *Ibid.,* p. 27.
38. *Ibid.,* p. 28.

CHAPTER SIX

1. F. Kersuady, *Norway 1940, op. cit,* p. 78.

2. Riste and Nokleby, *Norway 1940-45: The Resistance Movement, op. cit.,* p. 24.

3. *Ibid.,* p. 24.

4. Hove, Bjarne and Trygve M. Ager, *The Fight of the Norwegian Church Against Nazism, op. cit.,* p.17.

5. Riste and Nokleby, *Norway 1940-45: The Resistance Movement, op. cit.,* p. 17.

6. Riste and Nokleby, *Norway 1940-45: The Resistance Movement, op. cit.,* pp., 40-42.

7. Riste and Nokleby, *Norway 1940-45: The Resistance Movement, op. cit.,* p. 38.

8. *Ibid.,* pp., 40-43.

9. Gjelsvik, Tore, *Norwegian Resistance: 1940-1945.* (Great Britain, C. Hurst & Co. Publishers Ltd., 1979), p. 22.

10. *Ibid.* p. 23.

11. *Ibid.* p. 38.

12. *Ibid.* p. 36.

13. *Ibid.* p. 39.

14. Riste and Nokleby, *Norway 1940-45: The Resistance Movement, op. cit.,* pp., 40-41.

15. Hove, Bjarne and Trygve M. Ager, *The Fight of the Norwegian Church Against Nazism, op. cit.,* p. 82.

16. *Ibid.* p. 84.

17. *Ibid.* pp. 93-106.

CHAPTER SEVEN

1. Terdal, Harriet, *Our Escape From Nazi-Occupied Norway,* (Self published manuscript, 1971).

CHAPTER EIGHT

1. Sorvaag, Trygve, *Shetland Bus: Faces and Places 60 Years on,* (The Shetland Times Ltd, Lerwick, 2002), p. 12.

2. Howarth, David, *The Shetland Bus: A WW II Epic of Escape, Survival, and Adventure,* (London: Thomas Nelson and Sons Ltd., 1951), p.42.

3. *IIbid.* p. 43.

4. Ulstein, Ragnar, *The North Sea Traffic: Flight to War,* (Bergens Sjofartsmuseum, 1992), pp., 1-20. Note this book was published

in connection with the exhibition: "1940-1945, They Left Norway To Fight", presented in Scotland 1992 by the Orkney Norway Friendship Association.

5. Howarth, David, *We Die Alone: A WW II Epic of Escape and Endurance*, (Originally published in 1951 by the Macmillan Company, New York. First Lyons Press edition, 1999), pp., 1-31.

6. Sorvaag, Trygve, *Shetland Bus: Faces and Places 60 Years on, op. cit.*, pp., 12-26.

7. *Ibid.* p. 17.

8. Howarth, David, *The Shetland Bus: A WW II Epic of Escape, Survival, and Adventure, op. cit.*, pp., 68-77.

9. Sorvaag, Trygve, *Shetland Bus: Faces and Places 60 Years on, op. cit.*, p. 17.

10. *Ibid.* pp., 23-24.

11. *Ibid*

12. Ulstein, Ragnar, *The North Sea Traffic: Flight to War, op. cit.*, p.18.

13. Terdal, Harriet, *Our Escape From Nazi-Occupied Norway, op. cit.*, pp., 45-46.

14. Ulstein, Ragnar, *The North Sea Traffic: Flight to War, op. cit.*, p.18.

15. Howarth, David, *The Shetland Bus: A WW II Epic of Escape, Survival. And Adventure, op. cit.*, pp., 207-215.

16. *Ibid.* p. 210.

17. Riste and Nokleby, *Norway 1940-45: The Resistance Movement, op. cit.*, pp., 48-49.

18. *Ibid.* pp., 59-60.

CHAPTER NINE

1. Rohwer, Jurgen, *War At Sea: 1939-1945, op. cit.*, p. 54.

2. *Ibid.* p. 37.

3. *Ibid.* p. 38.

4. *Ibid.* pp., 41-44.

5. *Ibid.* p. 44.

6. *Ibid.* pp., 47-52.

7. *Ibid.* pp., 48-52.

8. *Ibid.* pp., 46-51/

9. *Ibid.* p. 50.

10. *Ibid.* pp., 51-53.

11. *Ibid.* pp., p. 80.

12. *Ibid.* p. 104.
13. *Ibid.* pp., 80-82.

CHAPTER TEN
1. Terdal, Harriet, *Our Escape From Nazi-Occupied Norway,* *op. cit.,* Chapter Seven in this book.

CHAPTER ELEVEN
1. Shirer, William L., *The Rise and Fall of the Third Reich - A History of Nazi Germany,* (New York: Simon & Schuster Paperbacks, 1960), p. 237.
2. *Ibid.* p. 237.
3. *Ibid.* p. 237.
4. Geffrey B. Kelly & F. Burton Nelson (Eds.), *Testament To Freedom: The Essential Writings of Dietrich Bonhoeffer,* (Harper San Francisco: A Division of Harper Collins Publishers, 1990), p. 21.
5. Shirer, William L., *The Rise and Fall of the Third Reich – A History of Nazi Germany, op. cit.,* p. 235.
6. Niemoller, Martin, *First Commandment,* (London, 1937), pp., 243-250.
7. Geffrey B. Kelly & F. Burton Nelson (Eds.), *Testament To Freedom: The Essential Writings of Dietrich Bonhoeffer, op. cit.,* p. 566.
8. Niemoller, Martin, *First Commandment, op. cit.,* pp., 243-250.
9. Michael, Robert, *Theological Myth, German Antisemitism, and the Holocaust: The Case of Martin Niemoller,* (Holocaust Genocide Studies, 1987): 2: pp., 105-122.
10. Armstrong, Karen., *HOLY WAR: THE CRUSADES AND THEIR IMPACT ON TODAY'S WORLD,* (New York: Anchor Books, 2001), p. 458.
11. Shirer, William L., *The Rise and Fall of the Third Reich – A history of Nazi Germany, op. cit.,* p. 239.
12. Gef
13. *First They Came*
14. Geffrey B. Kelly & F. Burton Nelson (Eds.), *Testament To Freedom: The Essential Writings of Dietrich Bonhoeffer, op.cit.,* pp., 3-17.
15. *Ibid.,* pp., 137-140.
16. See Eberhard Bethge, "Dietrich Bonhoeffer's and the Jews," in John D. Godsey and Geffrey B. Kelly, *Ethical Responsibility: Bonhoeffer's*

Legacy to the Churches (New York and Toronto: Edwin Mellen Press, 1981), pp. 43-96.

17. Geffrey B. Kelly & F. Burton Nelson (Eds.), *Testament To Freedom: The Essential Writings of Dietrich Bonhoeffer, op. cit.,* p. 133.

18. *Ibid.* p. 142.

19. *Ibid.* pp., 141-144.

20. *Ibid.* pp., 133-135.

21. *Ibid.* p. 18.

22. *Ibid.* pp., 18-20.

23. *Ibid.* pp., 19-20.

24. *Ibid.* p. 19.

25. *Ibid.* p. 25.

26. *Ibid.* p. 551.

27. Shirer, William L., *The Rise and Fall of the Third Reich – A History of Nazi Germany, op. cit.,* pp., 235-236.

28. *Ibid.* pp., 238-240.

29. *Ibid.* p. 238.

30. Geffrey B. Kelly & F. Burton Nelson (Eds.), *Testament To Freedom: The Essential Writings of Dietrich Bonhoeffer, op. cit.,* p. 531.

31. *Ibid.* p. 17.

32. *Ibid.* p. 15.

33. Bonhoeffer, Dietrich, *The Cost of Discipleship,* (New York: A Touchstone Book Published By Simon & Schuster, 1995), Note: Translated from the German *Nachfolge* first published 1937. Memoir by G. Leibholz, pp. 13-34.

34. Goldhagen, Daniel Jonah, ***A Moral Reckoning:*** *The Role of the Catholic Church in the Holocaust and its Unfulfilled Duty of Repair* (New York: Alfred A. Knopf, 2002), p. 166.

35. Ousby, Ian, *Occupation: The Ordeal of France: 1940–1944* (New York: St. Martins Press, 1998), pp., 192-197.

36. Armstrong, Karen, *HOLY WAR: THE CRUSADES AND THEIR IMPACT ON TODAY'S WORLD, op. cit.,* p. 469.

37. Stein, Leo (May 1941), NIEMOLLER SPEAKS! An Exclusive Report By One Who Lived 22 Months In Prison With The Famous German Pastor Who Defied Adolf Hitler, pp., 284-285, 301-302. The National Jewish Monthly.

38. Firm, Vergilius, *Pictorial History of Protestantism: A Panoramic View*

of Western Europe and the United States, (New York: Philosophical Library, 1957), p. 57.

39. The New York Times, 1/20/2005
40. Goldhagen, Daniel Jonah, *A Moral Reckoning: The Role of the Catholic Church in the Holocaust and its Unfulfilled Duty of Repair, op. cit.,* p. 226.

CHAPTER TWELVE

1. Gjelsvik, Tore, *Norwegian Resistance: 1940-1945, op. cit.,* p. 70.
2. Gilbert, Martin, *Kristallnacht: Prelude to Destruction, op. cit.,* p. 44.
3. Ousby, Ian, *Occupation: The Ordeal of France 1940-1945, op. cit.*
4. Gilbert, Martin, *Kristallnacht: Prelude to Destruction, op. cit.,* p. 124.
5. Ibid. p. 124.
6. Ibid. p. 124.
7. The New York Times. *Bertelsmann Offers Regret For its Nazi-Era Conduct, October 8, 2002*
8. Ibid.
9. Armstrong, Karen, *Holy War: The Crusades and Their Impact on Today's World,* op. cit., p.
10. The New York Times, *Hidden Synagogue Reveals Portugal's Dark Past,* December 26, 2005. This article describes a chance discovery of a small place of worship for Jews hidden behind a wall. This was used when Jews were forced to convert to Catholicism or risk being burned at the stake. The hidden place of worship was revealed when an ancient building was being remodeled in 2005, more than 500 years after the "Dark Past" associated with the inquisition.
11. Goldhagen, Daniel Jonah, *A Moral Reckoning: The Role of the Catholic Church in the Holocaust and its Unfulfilled Duty of Repair, op. cit.* p. 55

BIBLIOGRAPHY

Anderson, Arlow W., The Salt of the Earth: History of Norwegian Danish Methodism in America (Nashville, Tennessee, The Parthenon Press, 1962).

Armstrong, Karen, Holy War: The Crusades And Their Impact On Today's World (New York: Anchor Books, 1988).

Armstrong, Karen, A History of God (New York: Ballantine Books, 1993).

Barnett, Victoria, For the Soul of the People: Protestant Protest against Hitler (New York: Oxford University Press, 1992).

Cornwell, John, Hitlers Pope: The Secret History of Pius XII (New York: Anchor Books, 1988).

Goldhagen, Daniel Jonah, Hitler's Willing Executioners: Ordinary Germans and the Holocaust (New York: Alfred A. Knopf, 1996).

Goldhagen, Daniel Jonah, A Moral Reconing: The Role of the Catholic Church in The Holocaust and its Unfulfilled Duty of Repair (New York: Alfred A. Knopf, 2002).

Gjelsvik, Tore, Norwegian Resistance: 1940-1945 (London: C. Hurst & Company, 1979).

Harriman, Florence Jaffray, Mission to the North (New York, J.B. Lippincott Company, 1941).

Howarth, David, The Shetland Bus (New York, NY: The Lyons Press, 1951).

Howarth, David, We Die Alone (New York, NY: The Lyons Press, 1951).

Hoye, Bjarne and Trygve M. Ager, The Fight of the Norwegian Church against Nazism (New York, J.B. Lippincott Company, 1941).

Kelly, Geoffrey B. and F. Burton Nelson, eds, A Testament to Freedom: The Essential Writings of Dietrich Bonhoeffer. (revised edition) New York: Harper-Collins, 1955.

Kersaudy, Francois, Norway 1940 (Lincoln: University of Nebraska Press, 1987).

Kynoch, Joseph, Norway 1940: The Forgotten Fiasco (London, Airlife Publishing Ltd, 2002).

Macintyre, Donald, The Naval War Against Hitler (New York, Charles Scribner's Sons, 1971).

Midgaard, John, A Brief History of Norway (Oslo, Johan Grundt
   Tanum Forlag, 1963).
Popperwell, Ronald G., Norway: A Nation of the Modern World
   (London, Ernst Benn Limited, 1972).0
Riste, Olav and Berit Nokleby, Norway 1940-45: The Resistance
   Movement (Printed in Norway by Nor-Media A/S, 1994).
Rygg, A.N., Norwegians in New York: 1825 to 1925 (Brooklyn, N.Y.:
   Arnesen Press, Inc., 1941).
Stone, Ronald H, Niebuhr, Reinhold: Prophet to Politicians (New York:
   Abingdon Press, 1972).
Terdal, Harriet, Our Escape from Nazi-Occupied Norway (1965).